MARXISM
AND THE
IRRATIONALISTS

MARXISM
AND THE
IRRATIONALISTS

by

JOHN LEWIS

GREENWOOD PRESS, PUBLISHERS
WESTPORT, CONNECTICUT

Library of Congress Cataloging in Publication Data

Lewis, John, 1889-
  Marxism and the irrationalists.

  Reprint of the 1955 ed.
  1. Dialectical materialism. I. Title.
[B809.8.L48 1973]   335.4'11   72-6687
ISBN 0-8371-6494-X

146
L674m

Originally published in 1955 by Lawrence & Wishart Ltd,
London

Reprinted with the permission of Lawrence & Wishart Ltd

Reprinted by Greenwood Press,
a division of Williamhouse-Regency Inc.

First Greenwood Reprinting 1973
Second Greenwood Reprinting 1974

Library of Congress Catalog Card Number 72-6687

ISBN 0-8371-6494-X

Printed in the United States of America

81- 6001

CONTENTS

CHAPTER I

IDEALISM AND MATERIALISM, WHAT ARE THEY?

The Conflict in Philosophy

" ALL philosophical doctrines in general have always been created under the powerful influence of the social situation to which they belonged,"[1] and every philosopher has always been a representative of some definite social trend. But such doctrines do not merely reflect social existence, they play a definite role in history. They may " serve the interests of the moribund forces of society . . . hamper the development, the progress of society, " or they may " facilitate the over-throw of those forces which hamper the development of the material life of society." That is why the philosophical ideas current in any age should not be regarded as merely the speculation of academic persons ; they play their part in moulding our type of civilisation. As we think we live.

In periods of social advance and the increasing mastery of natural forces, philosophy will tend to be optimistic and to place trust in reason. Very different will be those philosophies which reflect periods of slow social decay. Philosophy is definitely related " to the passions which stir the country at a given time " and " even every transient state of feeling."[2] That is why in such periods pessimism and irrationalism pervade philosophy or there is a turning away from the incomprehensibilities and tragedies of life to some trans-cendental world of absolute goodness and pre-existent per-fection. Men in their disillusionment with human effort invoke the cosmic to rectify the evils of society and project the good they cannot achieve into the eternal.

Such are the dominant philosophies of the Western world today. But it is a too frequent error to pay attention to those philosophies which are current in the universities, the pulpits

[1] Chernyshevsky, *Selected Philosophical Essays.*
[2] *Ibid.*

I

and other accepted channels of thought and to overlook the constructive and advancing forms of thought, the harbingers of the age that is coming into being. It is true that " the ruling ideas of each age have ever been the ideas of the ruling class ", but there are other ideas arising among those who are in revolt against conditions, who represent the rival groups and classes which social development has called into being. Their philosophy will be in violent opposition to the ideas of the ruling class. As Marx said, " Before the proletariat fights out its battles on the barricades, it announces the coming of its rule with a series of intellectual victories." We have therefore the task of exposing and controverting those anti-social philosophies which are the allies of the existing order and whose role in history today is wholly negative and obstructive.

Such philosophies will be found to take the form of idealism. " Idealism ", says Professor Susan Stebbing, " is popularly understood to be the view that mind alone is real and that material bodies are in some sense or other to be regarded as states of, or elements in, consciousness—either the consciousness of human beings or of God."[1] But the term can be extended to all philosophies which regard ideas, principles, ideals, laws as having an independent existence of their own, so that the material world, historical events and human conduct in some way derive from them. Another form of idealism is the dualism which sets a pure world of mind over against a dead, mindless world of matter, the latter as much an abstraction as the former ; or the vitalism which postulates a life force as the agent of evolution and the source of all living and directive processes. Still another form of idealism is the philosophy that finds the ultimate reality on the one hand in sensations or observational data, or on the other hand in such concepts as " whiteness ", " squareness ", " duty ", " honesty " and so on, regarding all these " objects of thinking " as having a kind of existence of their own (or as the philosophers themselves would say, a *subsistence* of

[1] Stebbing, *Philosophy and the Physicists.*

their own). Many such philosophers would also regard the truths or propositions of logic and mathematics as constituting a special kind of reality discovered and apprehended by the mind of man. Such forms of idealism are somewhat akin to the philosophy of Plato, who believed that there existed a supra-physical world of realities which he called " Ideas ", eternal and unchangeable, the objects with which the definitions and universal truths of science are concerned. These for him were not " states " of the knowing mind, but objects distinct from and independent of the mind, about which it has knowledge. But later philosophers taught that objects of thought have no subsistence outside the thinking mind, and something rather like this is believed by many modern idealists.

Marxist Materialism

Perhaps the best way of understanding idealism is to contrast it with materialism in its Marxist form. · Marxist materialism totally rejects the existence of a supernatural, supersensible world standing over against this one, whether it consists on the one hand of ideas or concepts or principles existing in their own right, or on the other of disembodied spiritual beings which influence events in the physical world. It rejects too the derivation of the world, or of any phenomenon in the world, from some spiritual source which preceded it. There is thus only one world, the world in space and time that we know, a rich and varied world, an evolving changing world, in which thinking, feeling and loving have come to be the great realities, in which " the spiritual life of society "[1] is as real as the conditions of its material life. Dialectical materialism also holds that this world, and the life within it, including man and society, is fully penetrable by reason. It may be known with an ever greater degree of truth, both in its structure and laws, both in its behaviour and its processes of change.

We could sum this view up by saying that the underlying

[1] Stalin, *Dialectical and Historical Materialism.*

and continuing foundation of the universe is not mind or consciousness, but matter in its multiple and changing modes. The truth of this position, as we shall see, is not dependent upon the definition of matter in terms of any particular stuff, since science may continue to refine and alter its views of the ultimate constituents of matter. What is important is the belief that the external world, call it matter, substance, electricity or what you will, exists antecedently to and independently of the human mind, a Divine Mind, or any other conceivable mind.

The Suicide of Thought

It might be supposed that idealism would tend to be an optimistic faith, and from time to time it has been. But reflecting as it does, in its theory of the contrast between physical appearances and spiritual realities, the dualism of a divided society, it also reflects the sickness of that society. And thus do we find idealism in the doldrums.

Today there are people so mentally and emotionally over-whelmed, so distraught by the hydrogen bomb, by the fear of communism, by the uncertainties of existence, so bewildered and scared by radio propaganda and the Press, that " to them the present is intolerable and the future unthinkable. They have the courage neither to live nor to die. They see themselves driven to the edge of a yawning abyss. They can neither advance nor retreat. And so they naturally seek solace in mysticism, in an inward life that persuades itself of the unreality of the real. It is their emotional escape from the present, and they gladly seek refuge in the timeless."[1]

It might be useful to put on record a few of the many cries of despair now rising from our idealist philosophers. A writer for the Student Christian Movement, one of the most in-fluential ideological forces in our universities, declares that ours is " the rootless age. In our unawareness of foundations, unity and wholeness we are far worse than our remotest

[1] Prof. H. Levy in *The Communist Answer to the Challenge of Our Time*.

ancestors." And he launches into a fervent apologetic for the supernatural as the only way out.

Another speaking at a conference of university teachers admits among undergraduates, " a collapse of ultimate principles and ideals, an increasing area of subjective disruption, cynicism and lack of faith ",[1] and advocates a return to philosophy and instruction in philosophy in all universities as the way to a recovery of faith.

An American book, *Ideas Have Consequences*, by Richard Weaver, was reviewed at length recently in the B.B.C. Third Programme. Its theme is that our modern decadence is the fruit of a shallow empiricism—that is to say, of a philosophy which abandons the search for principles and lives by mere opinion, banishing the reality which is grasped by the intellect and accepting as reality only that which is perceived by the senses. " Most portentous of all, there appear diverging bases of value, so that our single planetary globe is mocked by worlds of different understanding." The remedy is to recover what he calls " the metaphysical dream ", by which he means a fixed framework of reference, a fundamental world view, to give coherence and meaning to life. This requires a realm of absolute, eternal realities, of fixed values, of goals towards which we can direct our efforts.

The argument is always the same. The mysteries and tragedies of a society which has had its day demand, for the idealist, not a realistic analysis of the moment of transition and a recognition that it is not the world that is in collapse, but capitalism, not man who is defeated and helpless but the social class which rules society today, but an escape into the supernatural and the transcendental, a pathetic cry for miraculous deliverance.

Another characteristic of the philosophical thought of our times is a profound disbelief in reason. How this could arise from the very nature of idealism is not at first clear. But the vice of idealism has always been to mistake the operations

---

[1] Synthesis in Education (*The Institute of Sociology*).

of the mind for a vision of reality ; to pass from the nature of thought to the nature of being. " The order and connection of ideas is the order and connection of things ", a rational scheme of things in the mind does not only *represent* reality, it *is* reality. The idealist is constantly postulating as already there, as already achieved, as, indeed, the ultimate reality behind the confusion of actual experience, the order and perfection and rationality of which men dream and which they seek behind the veil of illusion. But this turning away from the real environment to the mind of man who thinks about the environment started a movement that was bound to end in scepticism. For suddenly we see that we are contemplating only our own thinking. Our rationality is but the formal, empty outlines of a logical system, *not the natural world.* Our perceived world is not an objective, rational order, but only the world as forced into the framework of our systematising intellects. We can therefore never be sure whether the seeming rationality of the external world, if there is one, belongs to it or to some logical system we force upon it. So the idealism which tried to be objective is turned back on itself to sheer scepticism and subjectivity.

It is doubtful whether this has been a purely intellectual or theoretical development. In the early days of idealism it was the optimism of the nineteenth century that persuaded people that the world was as rational as they hoped it was. That is no longer possible for those who cannot see beyond the present order of society and a fatal contradiction emerges between the rational ideal of thought and the irrationality of the actual world.

And so faith in reason as a means of understanding reality and showing us how to control it and alter it peters out, and idealism itself ends in a violent attack upon the very possibility of knowing anything about nature or man, upon any philosophy which seeks to discover man's destiny and duty, even upon the very instrument of reason, which is declared to distort reality rather than reveal it.

But an attack upon systematic thought is treason to civilisation and throws away the chief safeguard against superstition. " Faith in reason is the trust that the ultimate natures of things lie together in a harmony which excludes mere arbitrariness. It is the faith that at the base of things we shall not find mere arbitrary mystery."[1]

Idealism and the External World

Let us now look at some of the more important idealistic tendencies in contemporary thought.

The most basic of these is still the much discussed view that what we perceive are always ideas and that we can never prove that there is a material world behind them. This was Bishop Berkeley's famous argument against eighteenth-century materialism. It has been said of this theory that it is equally impossible either to refute it or to accept it. This is not the case, and it has been refuted often enough. The truth is, however, that it is one of the most specious of philosophical arguments, and it is easier to be taken in by it than to see through it. In fact once one is tricked (that is the only possible term) into entertaining it, escape is not possible without a vigorous intellectual effort.

For this reason it is of little use merely to laugh it off or to attempt to refute it as Dr. Johnson did by kicking a large stone very vehemently. If the argument remains unrefuted, then the minds of many thoughtful people, even if they do not believe it, will have been subtly prepared for other, more credible but not less erroneous, idealistic conceptions.

Let us see how certain scientists and philosophers either draw very close to or even identify themselves with the Berkeleyan idealist position. Sir James Jeans says, " Our minds can only be acquainted with things inside themselves— never with things outside. . . . The Nature we study does not consist so much of something we perceive as of our perception."[2]

---

[1] Whitehead, *Science and the Modern World*.
[2] Jeans, *Presidential Address to the British Association*, 1934.

More than one scientist today falls into the same trap of declaring that we do not know physical objects but only states of consciousness. Bertrand Russell says : " Everything that we can directly observe of the physical world happens inside our heads and consists of mental events. The development of this point of view will lead us to the conclusion that the distinction between mind and matter is illusory." Russell thus dissolves the world into " mental events in the narrowest and strictest sense—any inference beyond percepts is incapable of being empirically tested." The mental, in perception, is thus held to be identical with the self-existent physical object. Sensations or percepts in a certain region of the brain are the ultimate facts.[1]

Professor Herbert Dingle, in his book *The Scientific Adventure*, is equally forthright in his confession of idealism. " What we know immediately is experience ; the world of material objects is what we (rightly or wrongly) infer from it."[2] The fallacy in such an inference, he says, is that first we say there must be a world of matter because we have experiences, and then we say that we have experiences because there is a world of matter which causes them.

We may digress to point out that if we were foolish enough to argue in this way we should indeed play right into the hands of idealism. But to say that there must be a world of matter because we have experiences, is to beg the question at the outset. That is what the idealist wants us to say, but of course we don't say it. We do not know experiences, we know physical objects, " knowledge unconditionally presupposes that the reality known exists independently of the knowledge of it, and that we know it as it exists in this independence," as Professor Prichard says.[3]

Dingle, who is professor of the history of science in University College, London, swings over completely to the position first

[1] Russell, *Our Knowledge of the External World*.

[2] Dingle, *The Scientific Adventure*.

[3] Prichard, *Kant's Theory of Knowledge*.

clearly expounded by Mach.[1] Science, he argues, aims " to organise the whole of *experience* into a rationally connected system, but unlike all previous philosophies, *it does not accept the world of material objects, but goes back to the original experiences* that led to the conception of that world for practical ends, and groups them differently."[2]

The pure philosopher does not really say anything very different when he says that the objects of philosophy belong wholly to the world of ideas. The minds of philosophers are normally directed upon the objects of a non-physical world and cannot easily bring attention to bear upon the contents of the physical one. The idealist scientist dwells on experiences in the mind, the transcendentalist philosopher on abstractions in the mind, and both reject knowledge of the material world.

[1] For an excellent summary of Mach's views and a critical treatment of them, see Cornforth, *Science versus Idealism.*
[2] Dingle, *loc. cit.* (our italics).

CHAPTER II

WHY BERKELEY WAS WRONG

Berkeley's Argument

BEFORE going any further it will be necessary to clear up the whole muddle about the theory that each mind perceives nothing but its own mental states. The idealist, or perhaps we should say the subjective idealist, who in the last resort discovers the objects of our knowledge to be ideas or sensations in our minds, argues something like this : When a hard, square, red object, such as a brick, is perceived, we are perceiving a collection of qualities, and we usually believe that the object, the brick in this case, is that which *has* these qualities. But all such qualities are only known to us as mental experiences of colour and the like. The red patch is really, for our minds, a sense experience, not a brick. If we smell a rose, we really smell an odour and that too is a sense experience. Even hardness and shape are tactile experiences. Let us call what we actually experience sense-data. It is clear that what we normally do is to interpret the sense-data as qualities of concrete objects and we say that we *perceive* the brick by *sensing its qualities*. The quality, we believe, requires a substance in which to inhere.

But does it ? The whole notion of substance is a myth, says the idealist. The *thing* is nothing more than the sum of its *experienced qualities*. There can be no possible proof of anything else. But since all qualities reside only in percipient minds, the object itself must do the same. In brief, the object is of the nature of an idea.

If that is so, the *idea* of a brick is not different from the idea of beauty, or squareness, or God. They are all mentally real, but not real in any other way. Nor is a brick more real than squareness, or squareness less real than a brick.

But the plain man at once points out a significant difference.

Not all ideas have the same status. Some are vividly and persistently held in our minds, *as if* these qualities inhered in some object before us, others are less objective, they are merely our ideas. The idealist grants this at once. He does not deny the existence of *objects which insist on being known* and which are persistently there. All that he is out to deny is that an experience of this kind requires a *material* universe. The experience, he argues, is not necessarily an experience of knowing *a material world*. It is only a peculiar kind of experience. It is still something mental. The real problem is what can be the *origin* of such an experience, if not a material object ? But since, even if matter existed, the idealist finds it hard to imagine how it would get across to something so different from itself as mind, why should not *something mental* be the cause of our experiences of collections of qualities ?

Idealists differ considerably as to what mental or " ideal " origin there might be for our perceptions. Bishop Berkeley, one of the ablest and the first of the modern idealists, held that the objects we perceive, not being of our own making, have a cause of their own, but that cause is not matter, but God. The only realities, then, are God, other spirits created by Him, and the various ideas or experiences which He has ordained to be apprehended in certain regular sequences. Idealism, however, need not believe in God and may instead simply rest in the ideal or mental character of all reality.

It will be seen that the upshot of the discussion is to disprove the existence of a material world and to suggest that the whole experienced universe is of the same nature as the mind. If that is the case, materialism is refuted and the principal objection to a religious explanation of the universe is removed. And that is precisely what the founder of modern idealism, Bishop Berkeley, intended. And very often it is precisely what our modern idealists have in mind as well.

Now what is the reply ? To strike a great stone with the foot and say " I refute it thus " is only to show that the theory has never even been understood.

The Refutation of Berkeley

We must do better than that. Yet refutation is simpler than might be supposed. When the idealist says that it is only our own mental states that we know, or that we certainly know them better than we know anything else, he is labouring under a misconception. Certainly to know a thing is to have an idea of it, but that does not mean that you only know the idea. Because you cannot be conscious of the material world without thinking about it, it does not follow that all you are conscious of is your thinking ! The fact that a known thing must, *as an element of knowledge,* be classed as an idea only means that when a thing is known it occupies a new relationship—the relationship of being known. But in thus assuming the status of an *idea,* as well as a material object, it does not by any means become identified with that idea. The object does not become an idea and nothing but an idea. Therefore whatever is known is not, just because it is thought about, itself of the nature of mind. The idealist confuses the thing apprehended with the act of apprehension. The thought of a thing must be in the mind, but the thing of which we are aware is not in the mind, and is therefore not mental. We thus vindicate a common-sense attitude to reality.

So far from mental experience shutting us up in pure subjectivism, mind is essentially that which possesses the characteristic of becoming acquainted with things other than itself. The idealists treat knowing in a way which flatly traverses our experience. As Whitehead says, " This experience knows away from and beyond our own personality— it is not a knowledge about our own personality."[1] Moreover it is not a passive perception of an un-get-at-able world, as if the observer were located in one of those glass observation chambers sunk in the sea. Knowledge is for action and results in action, and action means passing beyond the self into the world. That is why Marx said that " The dispute over the reality or non-reality of thinking which is isolated

[1] Whitehead, *Science and the Modern World.*

from practice is a purely scholastic question."[1] It is the success of our actions, argues Engels, that proves the correspondence of our perception with the objective nature of the objects perceived. " Practice ought to be the first and fundamental criterion of the theory of knowledge."

There *are* purely mental experiences, but they are quickly shown to be such by not standing up to the test of action. We then, rightly, call them illusions. If, on the other hand, any experience allows us to act upon it, *corrects* what was purely mental (i.e. illusory) by some sharp reaction or verifies the correctness of our perception by standing up to our activity, then we have no reason whatever to doubt its objectivity and materiality. E.g., a mirage does not allow us to slake our thirst, it vanishes as we approach. Real water is drinkable, can be splashed, objects float on it, it is wet, and so on. " Our knowledge of nature is an experience of activity." " If we are able to prove the correctness of our conception of a natural process by making it ourselves, bringing it into being out of its conditions and using it for our own purposes into the bargain, then there is an end of the Kantian incomprehensible ' thing-in-itself '. The chemical substances produced in the bodies of plants and animals remained just such ' things-in-themselves ' until organic chemistry began to produce them one after another, whereupon the ' thing-in-itself ' became a thing for us."[2]

In other words, there is a continual interaction between knower and known on the basis of his knowledge. What he knows enables him to act successfully. If his knowledge is not of the object as it is, is not correct, his action is unsuccessful and the result may be disastrous. Moreover, successful action changes the external situation and brings new facts before us, which we have to observe carefully and learn to know. This new knowledge immediately requires a new kind of action and so the process goes on.

Thus experience bears out the fact that we are very far

[1] Marx, *Theses on Feuerbach.*
[2] Engels, *Ludwig Feuerbach.*

from being locked up in the world of our own ideas. On the contrary, we are always finding out things about the world outside us and adjusting ourselves by action to its require- ments. Objectivity is of the essence of the experience.

The Consequences of Idealism

Bishop Berkeley thought that he had disproved materialism and proved idealism, and so do his twentieth-century disciples. As a matter of fact their arguments are the *reductio ad absurdum* of idealism and serve the useful purpose of showing us very clearly what follows from the *presupposition* of idealism. When we see that what follows is incredible we are forced to the conclusion that it is the *presupposition* that is indefensible.

If the consequences of a theory are manifestly contrary to fact, we must change the theory. If I think that a particular switch controls a particular light but when I turn it off the light continues to burn, then I know I was wrong about the switch, my supposition was incorrect.

Now the theory underlying idealism is that what we know are sensations, experiences, ideas, representations of objects, but not physical objects themselves. What follows from this ?

1. No material things exist in the universe, but only minds.

2. Each of us is shut up in his own mind with his own mental picture. There is no common public world existing independ- ently.

3. The world could not have existed before man appeared upon it. Where was it and what was it before it existed in minds ? Are the geologists and astronomers completely wrong when they describe its existence for some 3,000,000,000 years before man and his thoughts existed ?

4. Did my father exist before I came to know him ? Pre- sumably not, if to exist is to be perceived. Then I never had a father.

5. Did the rocket bomb go off in your head or in the street two hundred yards from your home ?

6. Look at a fish in an aquarium. Does the fish only know its sensations or is it aware of the tank and the objects in the

tank which it pursues or avoids ? *Is* there a tank ? *Are* there objects ? And if the fish sees you, do you exist only when and for as long as the fish sees you ? You *know* that there is a real world, a material environment for the fish, and that it senses it and reacts to it. Is there any less reason for accepting the physical environment around men ?

What do we conclude ? There must be something wrong with the theory that the real world cannot be known directly and that we only know mental representations existing in our minds. In other words, Berkeley has shown that " if anybody attempts to explain how material things exist and how we know them, by holding that we know mental representations of them, then he is next compelled to hold that there exist no such things at all, but only minds with sensations or ideas in them. He is compelled to hold that there exists no common public world of real things, and that mountains and railway engines are no more independently real entities than are toothaches. This is a conclusion we cannot accept, so that the original theory from which that conclusion is deduced must itself be abandoned."[1] That original theory is the presupposition, often taken for granted as unquestionable and obvious, that we know *things* only by knowing sensations which are purely mental, and then *inferring* the existence of things. It is precisely that assumption which is wrong. But if it is wrong because its consequences are contrary to fact, what other assumption can we make ? Surely that somehow or other we know the real world directly and not at second-hand. What we know is the real world and our knowledge of the world around us is not a vast illusion.

Knowledge not Passive

Behind the idealist approach is a curiously academic and contemplative attitude of mind, the existence of which we do not always realise (particularly if we are a bit academic and contemplative ourselves). Man is thought of as a mind examining its own mental processes and not an organism

[1] Sinclair, *Introduction to Philosophy*.

reacting to the world. Knowledge is thought of as a passive picture of things as they are, whereas actually knowledge is for action. The world is thought of as something which we infer beyond the veil of sensations, whereas actually we are part of it, it made us and we are making it with our hands.

What are ideas ? Not, surely, representations merely, but the way in which we become aware of and relate ourselves to our environment, the results of action, of purposeful struggle, technical progress, social achievements. If we regard man as a biological and social creature actively adjusting himself to an environment and through tools and co-operative activity adjusting that environment to human needs ; if we regard experience not as a picture in the mind, but as such a process of adjustment, and knowledge not as a copy of a real world, but as relating men to their environment and giving them power over it ; then the problem is transformed, and, set in these terms, presents no insoluble metaphysical problem.

All Knowledge is Relative

It must, however, be carefully noted just *what* is refuted. It is subjectivism, mentalism, but not the recognition of the relative character of all knowledge. This is a fact of the greatest importance, a fact unknown to the older materialists, and ignored by the uncritical. What idealism bequeathes to us as a permanent heritage, is what Lenin calls *the dialectical element in knowledge*, the recognition of the relativity of all knowledge, of the fact that it is strictly conditioned, that what we know of things *depends* on a multitude of particular circumstances. This is the truth behind the fact that we perceive only *through* sense-data. We perceive objects, but the *qualities* of objects which we perceive are *conditioned* in all manner of ways. Qualities do not merely *inhere* in substances but are given in the relationship of the observer to the object. In the object is " the permanent possibility of sensation ". That possibility is only realised under conditions, and not only the object, but *what* the conditions are, determine *what* the qualities are. Would-be Marxists sometimes think that everything in the idealist philosophies of Kant and his successors is complete nonsense, even vicious nonsense, and they themselves sometimes take the view that there is no problem of knowledge, that we simply see the objective material world just as it is and that is all there is to it. Vulgar materialism, which was severely criticised by Marx, conceived of our perceptions and ideas simply as the image produced in our consciousness when those bodies impinged on our sense organs. But in point of fact we only know those aspects of reality which have been revealed to us in our actual dealing with nature and that depends on all sorts of historical, technological and sociological factors. We gain our knowledge, in other words, not by the passive reception of impressions but by altering our environment in accordance with our needs. The fact that consciousness does not consist in a passive reception of impressions but is an activity was clearly understood by the great idealist philosophers from Kant onwards, but their mistake was to conceive this as an activity of the mind alone, and not as a mental activity which accompanies and directs a physical activity. This is why Lenin says that it is its *one-sidedness* which vitiates idealism, i.e., the fact that it conceives the active side only abstractly, as an activity of pure thinking. " Philosophical idealism is nonsense only from the standpoint of a crude, simple and metaphysical materialism. On the contrary, from the standpoint of dialectical materialism philosophical idealism is a one-sided, exaggerated, swollen development of one of the characteristic aspects or limits of knowledge."[1] This aspect of knowledge is the fact that it is always relative to the knower and to the conditions of knowing.

Knowledge is Highly Selective

This is clearly seen if we consider a very simple example.[2] When we consider our sense organs the remarkable thing

[1] Lenin, *On Dialectics.*
[2] For this illustration I am greatly indebted to W. A. Sinclair's *Introduction to Philosophy* and to his *Conditions of Knowing.*

about them is *how little they do in fact detect*. Our eyes only react to wave-lengths between certain defined limits. They do not react to other electro-magnetic vibrations. We can say that our eyes are blind to very nearly all that surrounds us. The same is true of hearing, except that the waves are in air (and in liquids and solids) and are not electro-magnetic waves. Our ears are deaf to very nearly everything. The same applies to all our other sense organs. They select for our attention only sections of the environment. This is very different from the thoroughgoing idealist position which regarded the richness of experience as purely subjective and as having nothing in the real world corresponding to it. The contrary is true, the real world is almost unbelievably rich and complicated. What we experience is only a fragmentary selection of the real world. We do not experience anything like the whole of reality, but only scraps of it, just as a wireless set picks up one programme out of dozens in the air.

We have therefore passed beyond the idealist position that the content of sensation is purely mental and subjective. Instead we have come to the opposite conclusion, that the real world includes all that we sense *and much more*, it is all that I experience it to be, and what other people in other circumstances experience it to be, and what animals and insects experience it to be, and a very great deal more besides. " The reason why we have different experiences is not that each of us has a private and subjective picture but that each of us picks out and attends to only a part of the immensely rich and complex world in which we find outselves."[1] But the sensation of the subject is not simply an aggregate of definite physiological acts of perception determined by its bodily organisation, but is always only *relatively* a direct knowledge of the world, since it is the apprehension of an individual in a particular historical situation. The direct perception of actuality at a given stage of social development, by a member of a given class, is affected by the whole of the past experience of society and of that class. Direct perception

[1] Sinclair, *Introduction to Philosophy.*

becomes knowledge permeated by past experience and conditioned by the social and technological stage of development. In fact it might be said that the senses of man develop and are perfected along with the development of social-historic practice.

Thus knowledge comes to be conditioned not only by the senses and the limitations of the technical approach, but by our interests and purposes. The world around us as we experience it, is not just simply " there " as we experience it. It is very largely made by us in the sense that we select and group together certain aspects in relation to the kind of activity we engage in, the progress of science and the stage in social development we have reached.

Abstract Rationalism Unscientific

Clearly if all thinking is thus conditioned, truth will always be partial and open to revision; but there is no reason on that account to despair of the tentative methods of scientific investigation and collapse into a bewildered scepticism. Partly, this is a reaction from the all-or-nothing view that will be content with nothing short of a total and finished transcription of reality. Philosophy has been obsessed with this demand for an intellectual short cut to complete and absolute knowledge, and has tended to discard the method of slow and stable advance, of gradually consolidated gains, in its impatience to reach its absolute by some brief formula, some all-compassing declaration covertly assuming its conclusion— the greatest vice in thinking. Thus certain forms of idealism have asserted that the existence of a rational universe is *implied* in human thinking, as though thought, and our existing technique of thinking at that, our defective logic, were the very index of reality and the only index. It thus seeks to prove the external by delving into the internal and concludes by deriving the order, connection and very existence of material things from the existence, order and connection of a logical system of ideas. This turning away from the real environment to the mind of man who thinks about his environment is bound to end in scepticism ; for scientific knowledge and its achievements are necessarily a much more chaotic and patchy thing than the tidy abstract rationalism that reaches its goal by vaulting over all the awkward facts.

Impossibilism

There is, however, another source of the doctrine of the limitation of human knowledge, so characteristic of contemporary thinking. Maurice Cornforth has pointed out that it turns up everywhere and has indeed " grown into a central tendency of modern bourgeois ' scientific ' ideology. This tendency might well be named ' impossibilism '. Its typical attitude is expressed in the single words, ' Impossible '."[1] " The fact is that capitalism has reached its limits, and this is what is being expressed in the pervading subjectivist and relativist philosophy, which penetrates every sphere of thought and activity. This philosophy is the typical ideological expression of the general crisis of capitalism. It expresses the state of the capitalist world as it appears to the denizens of that world just as faithfully as the liberal philosophy of the mid-nineteenth century expressed the rising phase of industrial capitalism."[2]

Yet once again we must beware of onesidedness, of falling over backwards into a complete denial of objective truth and the assertion that all we know are fictions or symbols created by our own minds. However relative our knowledge may be to the conditions under which we know, whatever properties and laws we discover, are really there and are as accurately recorded as the circumstances allow. The results are true as far as they go. This is less than naive realism claims when it asserts that we know objects as they really and completely are in themselves, but very much more than is allowed by sceptical idealism which declares that we cannot be sure of anything at all outside our own mental states. In other words, each recorded observation and discovery is a step forward to

[1] Cornforth, *Communist Review*, July, 1953.
[2] Cornforth, *Dialectical Materialism and Science*.

absolute objective knowledge. The steps of our advancing science are partial and limited, but they advance into fuller and fuller truth.

The Infinite Potentiality of Matter

Now we have hitherto been discussing only our knowledge and its conditions. But it is already obvious that we cannot separate (though we can distinguish) knowledge and its object. When we say that under certain conditions of temperature and light a certain substance is a colourless fluid, we are stating the limits of our knowledge at that moment and at the same time describing the object, not absolutely, but relatively. If we lower the temperature, the same substance may become hard and opaque. This extends the limits of our knowledge and adds new properties under new conditions to the object. This is a very simple example, but modern science is at one with Marxism in stressing *the great variability and the infinite potentiality of things*, which are not neat bundles of fixed qualities, but ever-changing complexes with explosive possibilities and a great range of properties, only few of which we at present know.

So that we no longer say : This is a hard, square, red object, but: This is an object which in this particular light, at this particular temperature, from here is a square, red object, and, in relation to what I am scratching it with, it is hard.

That, of course, is simple enough. But it is not quite so simple when you begin to organise things into different patterns or combinations. Suddenly entirely new and unpredictable properties emerge. Chemical compounds have quite different properties from the elements which combine to form them. Hydrogen is a gas, oxygen is a gas, but their combination in certain proportions is water. Organic substances have quite different properties from inorganic and yet may be synthesised from the inorganic. Protoplasm performs a synthesis which we cannot as yet perform in the laboratory ; it builds organic substances first into proteins and into new protoplasm which exhibits the characteristics of life—it respires, it reproduces itself, it moves, it excretes, it responds to stimuli.

Life is simply the property of a particular pattern or combination of previously non-living parts, but its reality and novelty are undeniable.

The relativity principle thus becomes the principle of emergence, the principle of the infinite potentiality of matter. It completely shatters the older materialist view that matter was a limited and almost altogether known affair which was certainly predictable in all its reactions and as certainly incapable of the transition from non-living to living. In so far as idealism insists that we do not know anything completely but only under the peculiarly limited conditions of each particular experience of knowing, it helps us, without mentalism or magic, to loosen up the rigidities of an earlier materialism.

But once again note that this is a statement about our knowledge and not only about matter. Knowledge, we see, is not a " reading off " of the specification of an object, but a statement of the result of a particular relationship between the knower and the known at a particular moment and under the unique conditions of that moment. Knowing is a two-way business in which the way I approach what I know, what I do in order to find out what it is, the conditions of my knowing, are important, as well as what the object is in itself.

The Error of Relativism

But when we see that knowledge is thus always relative we must not fall into the " relativism " which denies any real knowledge of the world at all. For it is a genuine aspect of the real world which we know in such relative knowledge. Thus every verified bit of relative knowledge " is a step forward to ' absolute objective knowledge '." " Human reason then in its nature is capable of yielding and does yield the absolute truth which is composed of the sum-total of relative truths." " Relative truths represent approximate reflections of an object which exists independent of humanity . . . these reflections continually approach the truth."[1]

There is a sharp distinction between this form of relativism which has no sceptical significance and the pure relativism of much idealist philosophy and even of many scientists who have fallen under the influence of idealism. This latter view denies all possibility of reaching the objectively true, the reality behind appearance, and in principle sees no distinction between the true and the false. On the basis of such a view, truth and error, objective fact and illusion, scientific knowledge and superstition emerge as equally valid. The inevitable incompleteness of knowledge and the inevitability of error and partiality, are declared to be a proof of the complete subjectivity of any scientific statement whatever. Any attempt to see in the truth of science the reflection of a reality independent of man is held to be entirely vain.

Scepticism and its Consequences

It may be useful to see what consequences flow from these sceptical philosophies.

1. Professor Herbert Dingle argues that the sole purpose of science is to organise and arrange sense data or data of observation, not to understand reality. All that reason does is to piece together the bits of experience, laws being created by the mind to bring these experiences together in a rational system.

Any set of experiences can therefore be treated in the same way and they will be equally valid, for their validity lies wholly in the rationality of the system into which they fit, not in their correspondence to objective reality.

It therefore becomes " impossible for the scientist, if he is to remain scientific, to explain away any experience as a negligible phantom of a diseased mind. It has as legitimate a place as any other experience among the data from which we build up our separate world-pictures."[2] We must therefore be content today with a series of such organised sets of

---

[1] Lenin, *Materialism and Empirio-Criticism.*
[2] Dingle, *The Scientific Adventure.*

experiences, among which there can be no possibility of conflict. It is quite clear that we have here a wide-open door for
any kind of belief, based on any kind of experience, including
those which most psychologists would characterise as delusions.

2. A somewhat similar position is taken up by G. Ardley in
his book *Aquinas and Kant, The Foundations of the Modern Sciences*.
His thesis is that all science is an imaginative reconstruction
of sense data which makes no claim to be true. It is a kind
of castle in the air. "What we comprehend about the
universe is precisely that which we put into the universe to
make it comprehensible." This being so, science makes no
claim at all to know reality. It dwells in a world of its own
and enjoys autonomy therein. Science does not pretend to
tell us anything about ultimate reality, about God, man, free
will, history or morals. It cannot contradict religion and
religion cannot contradict science, because science makes no
claim to describe reality.

Reality is approached by another road which does not use
the schemes, or categories, or forms of thoughts by means of
which science organises its material. This approach is via the
philosophy of Aristotle and Aquinas which discovers the real
nature of things by the orthodox methods of traditional
philosophy.

This is ingenious. If science is true it contradicts Catholic
theology, indeed its whole method proceeds along quite other
lines and by contrast the intellectual procedure of theology
looks ridiculous. However, if science is not true at all, no
such reflection falls upon theology, which may be accepted as
the only way to a true knowledge of reality.

3. Dingle also argues that if we try to explain the data of
science in terms of the structure of an external world, rather
than by merely linking experiences together in a rational order,
then the picture we get of such a world will be an irrational
one. The only way, therefore, to avoid a belief that reality
is fundamentally irrational is to give up looking for it at all
and be content with any scientific concepts, or formulæ, or
laws which harmonise the data.

But surely all that this means is that modern science is incompatible with the over-simplified picture of a physical world composed of solid interacting particles whose motions were wholly determined by simple mechanical laws. This is now clearly seen to be an inadequate picture, in fact no " picture " suffices today to explain the constitution and behaviour of matter on the sub-microscopic level. But the world, certain of whose aspects are describable by modern physical theories is not itself irrational because it is found to consist of processes rather than things, " something more like a candle flame than a stone." All that this means is that nature is not a machine, the parts of which are the same whether in the machine or separate from it and can exist independently of it. What we get at each lower level is something different from what we are analysing. The molecule is the smallest particle of what we are dividing. When we divide it we don't get a smaller portion of the same stuff—the stuff simply disappears, and we get something quite different, as when water breaks down into hydrogen and oxygen.

This is not to discover irrationality at the heart of things.

On the contrary, law still holds, system binds things to-gether ; granted the same conditions, the same effects can be depended upon ; there is uniformity, interconnectedness ; and is not this intelligibility ? Neither is there a blank wall of inscrutability. There are still endless things to find out. Nature continues to reveal itself. Endless novelties appear. Science is vindicated in and manifested in man's concrete achievements. All our knowledge is of order, pattern, con-stants and uniformities in the relations of material phenomena. It is no longer supposed to be the discovery of " essences " or unalterable natures ; nor is it the perception of " lumps " of matter—matter to be material has not to consist of small hard particles, but merely to exist independently of minds.

It is unnecessary therefore to regard the new physics as leading either to a scepticism of the intellectual instrument or to the discovery that reality is irrational. Matter on the sub-microscopic level is not "pictureable" in the old way, but that is not to say that it is either non-existent or irrational. The reign of law is not overthrown. Nature is dependable. The universe is consistent and orderly. It is these conceptions which have *made* modern science and they are unquestionably of fundamental importance for modern civilisation.

Endless Approximation to Truth

We can thus combine, and every scientist doing his real job always does combine, a real acknowledgment of deeper and deeper discovery of the nature of the actual material world and its laws, on the one hand, and a frank recognition of the partiality and relativity of that knowledge on the other. The conditionality, the relativity, of every different step of knowledge of actuality, are engendered by the limitations belonging to each given stage of social practice and dictate our notions of the object. So that thought is not able finally to grasp truth as a whole though it continually approaches it.

" The world and its laws are absolutely knowable to man, but they can never be completely known."[1]

The inevitable and necessary abstractions of scientific theory may even from time to time cause it to lose touch with actuality. Its limitations must necessarily contain the possibility of error. But the limitations of the historic conditions, the limitations of the particular world outlook of any age are *historical* limitations ; they are not based on any fundamental principle rendering knowledge by the very nature of things impossible. They can therefore be progressively overcome at a higher level of historic development. Moreover the knowledge we accumulate and verify in social practice is gradually built up into the law-system of scientific theory and enters into the iron inventory of permanent scientific knowledge.

Thus in the development of scientific knowledge a unity

[1] Lenin, *Materialism and Empirio-Criticism.*

of absolute and relative truth is realised.[1] On the one hand dialectics as a theory of knowledge admits the endlessness of the attainment of knowledge, never making absolute even its truest reflection, for if it did so it would cease to express the dialectics of the material world and thus lose its power of " guidance for action " ; on the other hand dialectics admits the absoluteness, the truthfulness of the process of scientific knowledge as a whole and the presence of portions of absolute truth in every scientific proposition, because it sees in it a firm basis for the assured advance of human achievement.

The refusal to admit the unity of absolute and relative truth leads inevitably to the admission of one of these to the exclusion of the other, leads either to the changing of theory into dogma, or to a direct denial that theory is a reflection of actuality and therefore capable of furnishing a scientific basis for the transformation of actuality.

[1] See Lenin, *Materialism and Empirio-Criticism*, p. 107.

CHAPTER III

THE REFUTATION OF MECHANISTIC MATERIALISM

Russell on the Physiology of Perception

A POSITION almost identical with that of idealism has been reached by certain physiological materialists. This position has been expounded, for instance, by Bertrand Russell. They point out that our only evidence for the existence of an external world is given by certain sensations which are themselves the result of nervous impulses activating certain cells in the brain. These nerve impulses are set up by purely physical stimuli—heat, wave motion, pressure, applied to certain nerve endings in the skin, eye, ear and so forth. Now we have no reason at all to assume that the *mental end-effect* produced in a brain cell at the end of a long chain of physical or physiological events is in any way *like* the original stimulus, any more than the explosion of a cartridge is like the finger which pressed the trigger. The physiology of the human body and the brain, it is argued, shuts us up with mental end-effects. " Everything that we can directly observe of the physical world," says Bertrand Russell, " happens inside our heads and consists of mental events. The development of this point of view will lead us to the conclusion that the distinction between mind and matter is illusory." Thus a purely materialistic view ends up as something indistinguishable from idealism. But by a curious inconsistency, as Whitehead has pointed out, these same people who express themselves as though bodies, brains and nerves were the only real things in an entirely imaginary world base all their evidence on the experimenters' perception of another person's body. But our evidence for the bodies we experiment upon and dissect in order to build up our science of physiology is of exactly the same type as, but weaker than, our evidence for the external world we are asked to deny. These materialists are treating bodies on materialist principles in order to treat all the rest of the world on idealist principles, and it won't do. An excellent example, we may remark, of what Bosanquet called " the meeting of extremes in contemporary philosophy."

We have already indicated the reply. If we are quite sure that these end-effects are obtained by a physical stimulus falling on a specific nerve-ending or sense organ which can be fully described, as of course can the physical stimulus and its origin ; if we are quite sure about the optic and other sensory nerves which we have dissected out and experimented with, and of the brain with its nerve cells, localised functions, visual and auditory areas, etc., all the result of endless experiments ; we are surely pretty certain about the existence of at any rate that much of the external world. And if we find no reason to doubt that, why doubt the rest ? It is a most curious argument and a surprising one for so acute a logician as Bertrand Russell. The fact that we have knowledge of our nervous systems, our brains and so on is used to establish the conclusion that we do not possess knowledge of the external world in which are to be found brains and nervous systems.

What we know is said to be perhaps " symbolic " of the real world which excites sensational " signals " in the brain. But if what I know directly is in my head we cannot compare it at all with its unknown cause. It cannot give us the faintest indication, symbolic or otherwise, of what that cause is.

The plain fact is that it is only because Russell knows *first* that there are external objects and proceeds to argue on the assumption of their existence, basing his whole argument on what is going on in this real, material world, that he is able to infer that there are private sense data and then to attempt to prove that nothing else exists !

But the argument is, from the other end, so to speak, only Bishop Berkeley all over again. It is not a physiological argument for mentalism but a philosophical argument, and to that we have already replied. Russell, like the Bishop, confuses perceiving and the thing perceived, perception and the brain event. He fails to understand that we do not perceive perceptions, or even brain events ; we perceive objects.

Biology and Perception

To the biologist no such doubts as to the existence of the external world are likely to occur because, unless he is a very bad biologist, he is concerned all the time not with a dead specimen on a dissecting board, in whose anatomy he is interested, but with a living organism functioning in an external environment adapted to that environment and constantly reacting to it. The biologist works on two major assumptions, firstly that the animal is *aware* of its environment and has a most elaborate apparatus of sense organs and responsive mechanisms to keep it aware and to make swift reaction possible ; secondly, he assumes that his organisms do function in relation to a real world and do know a great deal of it, enough of it to react satisfactorily, and survive. In fact if an animal is insufficiently aware of it the external world will, in the form of the inanimate environment or living enemies, very speedily terminate its existence.

The biologist also believes that while even the most primitive organisms possess this awareness and power of response, the most complex, including mammals and man, have developed awareness and response to an altogether amazing degree. Moreover, he knows that in the case of man, we have not only a very subtle and skilful control of behaviour in relation to environmental demands but foresight and self-awareness and organised social life on the basis of the power to make and improve tools, of which there is no evidence among the simpler forms of animal life.

No biologist, for whom an animal exists in relation to a real environment and reacts to it through awareness and the power to know it, can be either a mentalist denying the external world or a mechanistic materialist, except when he is contradicting his own scientific thinking by a false philosophy.

The significance of the biological approach is immense. It is at one and the same time a refutation of idealism and a refutation of that form of materialism which excludes mind from the universe. Constrained by its own subject matter, its own experience and experiment, biology holds together what man has too often put asunder, mind and matter.

Dualism as a form of Idealism

What this approach is mainly concerned to deny, therefore, is that strange dualism which is more often the outcome of idealist thinking than the far less acceptable view that we are shut up in our own thinking and can never get beyond our thoughts to a world outside them. This latter may well be the logical conclusion of many forms of idealism and it proves the falsity of the initial assumptions of which it is the conclusion ; but the more common form which idealism takes is dualism, not today the crude dualism of mind and matter, but the splitting of nature into two divisions, the nature apprehended in awareness and the nature which is the cause of awareness. What we experience is sensation, is the greenness of the trees, the song of the birds, the hardness of stone—what is supposed to cause this is the conjectural system of molecules and electrons which is nothing like the effects in consciousness which it produces. The whole notion really implies that the mind only knows its own states, but that it requires something from outside itself to originate those states. Thus we have two realities, an appearing reality confined to the mind, and a non-appearing reality which lies beyond consciousness and is only known by the mysterious effects it creates in consciousness. Thus the totality of being is divided into *a reality which does not appear and appearances which are not real.*

This hopeless position indicates something seriously wrong with its initial presupposition. In fact it reflects a mechanistic physics and can therefore only be escaped if nature is conceived as a single unitary system, if we realise that there is only *one* nature, given us in perception, that knowledge of it is one and the same from rudimentary sensations to advanced scientific hypotheses, which are based on the data of perception. Everything perceived is to be found in nature. All we know of nature is in the same boat to sink or swim together. In such a world every fact is a result of the *relatedness* of things, and every fact is a *process* rather than a static entity. The perception of a green object is something going on in a particular place involving eyes, retinas, light, brains, objects possessing a particular kind of surface and so on. Seeing is not just something in the mind, but something in the room, in the vicinity. Mental phenomena are part of the natural world, not private experiences in our minds. Qualities sensed occur under definite natural conditions ; just as any chemical or electrical phenomenon may be relied upon to occur granted the requisite conditions.

A New Conception of Nature

This involves a new conception of nature. It is not a soundless, colourless concatenation of moving molecules, devoid of mind, values and ethical significance—the ultimately real of dualism ; on the contrary all qualities belong to it—under specific conditions. Atoms are capable of many strange things when complexly organised. This being so you never go behind experience to find something more real. Actual entities, including (in those cases where man is involved) consciousness, purpose and valuation, are all that there is, and they are always in process of development and change, bringing something new into the world, enriching it by fresh creation. The crux of this view is a change in the concept of substance from something static, with fixed properties inhering in it, to something dialectical, developing, moving, embracing contradictory, interpenetrating aspects.

All that plays any part in physics is the process itself and it does not in the least matter what the " something " is in which the process takes place.

The old metaphysical notion of substance is no longer made use of, since everything in the physical universe is in flux and everything has to be stated in terms of the law of the process. Hence the world picture is a dynamic one. A hydrogen atom does not exist in a static sense ; it happens. We don't first need a substance, so that secondly something can happen to it. " In place of cold, dead, rigid matter we have the restless flow, the crossing and recrossing of billions upon billions of actions, which together, however, do not result in chaos, but in a cosmos of a symmetry, order and regularity."[1] The whole of existence is thus resolved into perpetual becoming or happening. We are thus reading a new and richer significance into what is meant by existence and causality. This new conception does not in the least affect either the material reality or the construction of a logical connection between the various parts or partial processes of world events. All that it means, in terms of physics, is that there are " elements " in the sub-atomic, microscopic world that have no familiar counterparts in the macroscopic world, and in particular that all static models of atomic structure are done away with.

Mechanistic Views Unscientific

The materialist who, believing only in the physiological mechanism leading to brain events, so surprisingly ends up as an idealist does not, of course, anticipate that this will prove the inevitable conclusion of his argument. He sets out to prove only that mind does not exist, that there is nothing properly to be called real but matter, which is limited to predictable chemical and physiological effects. For him, if consciousness occurs at all, it is either a sort of shadow cast by the brain or in some other way consistent with the complete dependence of mind on matter. Consciousness, in that case, becomes a product without consequences, as a chalk mark left by drawing with a piece of chalk on a board is an effect left by the pasage of the chalk but has, as a mark, itself no effect on the chalk nor on the hand which moves the chalk. This for most materialists is the conclusion of the argument, and it is the classical position of what is often called mechanistic materialism but more generally known simply as the materialist philosophy.

Marxism has always strenuously opposed this form of

[1] Bavink, *The Anatomy of Modern Science.*

materialism on the ground that it is in flat contradiction of the evidence to reduce life and consciousness to chemistry. Marxism does not deny the reality of either life or mind. It asserts, however, that they are functions of highly organised matter on the organic lievel.   The new conception of qualitative difference between one level and another is not entirely a matter of quantity but of dynamic pattern.   When Needham speaks of " levels of organisation " with their own regularities and qualities not reducible to those belonging to lower levels of organisation, he does less than justice to the qualitatively unique types of *movement* responsible for these differences. Pattern there is, but it is a pattern constantly moving in a definite and rhythmical way.   This is the real link between quantity and quality.   Life is an excellent example.   What differentiates a living body from one just dead is that in the living animal certain rhythmical processes and changes are going on which are absent from the dead body.

These differences are not, as the emergent evolutionists often describe them, inexplicable jumps which we must simply accept.   They are in no way inscrutable or immune from scientific analysis or comprehension, even though the task of analysing them is an endless one.

The Theory of Levels

We conclude that the levels of life and mind are not *reducible* to physical and chemical differences only.   " The vital processes of an organism, the development of society, the thought of man, are all qualitatively unique processes, which it is quite impossible to reduce to simple movements of particles."[1]

The Marxist does not attribute these special characteristics to the infusion of a vital principle into matter from the realm of mind or spirit.   He claims that in the realm of nature are to be found different patterns of movement in an ascending series.   " From ultimate physical particle to atom, from atom to molecule, from molecule to colloidal aggregate, from aggregate to living cell, from cell to organ, from organ to

[1] Shirokov, *Textbook of Marxist Philosophy.*

body, from animal body to social association, the series of organisational levels is complete."

We thus exclude from biology all factors that are not accessible to scientific investigation and are conceivable only by imagining something akin to the directive activity of mind operating at a non-mental level, i.e. without a nervous system.

At the same time there are undoubtedly biological laws of a specific kind and of a higher order than that of the laws of physics. A third level comprises the sphere of psychology. Of course it cannot be doubted that the realm of biology is dependent upon the physical and chemical, but this does not obviate the necessity of establishing the laws of biological levels as such.

Dialectically, the behaviour of matter on this level leads to an expansion of the system of concepts and laws of physics and in particular to a new significance to the rhythmic *pattern* of events or mode of motion in distinction from mere quantity. Biology more than anything else has brought to the fore the importance of laws concerning organic systems as a whole, so that while " organic life is impossible without mechanical, molecular, chemical, thermal, electrical and other changes, the presence of these collateral forms does not exhaust the essence of the main form."[1] It still has in addition to these indispensable and constituting movements its own unique character. Breathing and digestion comprehend a whole range of chemical changes. But in none of these is included the specific quality of an organism, its uniqueness. The movement characteristic of an organism is the ceaseless changing of organic substances—a process of combustion, dissolution and renovation of living matter, a process of assimilation and synthesis, whereby the fabric of the body is continuously being woven. These biological changes contain within themselves those other forms of movement which are collateral to the unique living processes of the organism. In the interlacing of a number of distinct and subordinate physical and chemical processes there is always a determined species

[1] Shirokov, *Textbook of Marxist Philosophy.*

of movement which embraces all the others, subordinates them to itself, and is characteristic of the thing as a whole. The physico-chemical description of isolated and subordinate processes, on which the whole depends, do not, considered in themselves, explain the unique behaviour of the biological phenomenon. It thus becomes the essential task of biology to find the law-system of the organism, a task hitherto hardly contemplated by " mechanistic " biology.

If we subject a living organism to a purely external analysis into its elements we shall find nothing except physico-chemical processes. But this by no means denotes that life amounts to a simple aggregate of these physico-chemical elements. The particular physico-chemical processes are connected in the organism by a new form of movement. Thus in the organic realm there exist *higher levels of order and organisation*, compared to those in the inorganic.

It is in this new type of organisation and movement that the quality of the living thing lies. The new in a living organism, not being attributable to physics or chemistry, arises as a result of the new synthesis, of the new *pattern* of physical and chemical movements. This synthetic process whereby out of the old we proceed to the emergence of the new is understood neither by the mechanists nor by the vitalists.

The Higher is based on the Lower

Of course the more complex organisation which manifests the quality of being alive includes in itself elements of the simpler. Men cannot exist without purely physiological processes that are not in themselves human, and physiological processes cannot go on without purely chemical and physical processes. But here is the point : the elements of the old by being subordinated to the new system, by entering into the new synthesis, themselves become something new. Physico-chemical processes within an organism undergo a radical change. " The unique conditions of every chemical process within an organism are such that this process reaches results that under inorganic conditions are impossible."[1] Thus *quality*, as the special system of a given whole, as the unique form of movement, lays its imprint on those elements from which it emerged itself. The task of science does not lie in reducing a whole to the parts, as though the differences of qualities were only a subjective appearance which we must accept until we reach the real explanation, it does not lie in " the untying of qualitative knots ", as the mechanists put it, nor on the other hand in studying a whole as such, but in the disclosure of the relations, the pattern of movements, peculiar to each quality in its emergence and development. Engels discussing the relation of the different sciences with each other put it thus :—

" By calling physics the mechanics of molecules, chemistry the physics of atoms, biology the chemistry of proteins, I wish to express the transition of each one of these sciences into the other and therefore the connection, the continuity and also the distinction, the break between the two fields. Biology does not in this way amount to chemistry yet at the same time is not something absolutely separated from it. In our analysis of life we find definite chemical processes. But these latter are now not chemical in the proper sense of the word ; to understand them there must be a transition from ordinary chemical action to the chemistry of proteins, which we call life."[2] Just as life in its simplest form is characteristic of the colloidal condition of proteins known as protoplasm, and has the altogether new power in nature of synthesising new protoplasm from organic acids, so protoplasm organised in a living cell follows this power of organic growth with the new powers of reproduction, of self-repair, of response to stimulus. At a higher level still, specialised cells concern themselves wholly with registering impressions from the environment and bringing about the activation of muscles which secures an appropriate response. These nerves are called receptors and effectors. Finally a complex organisation of nerve cells is

[1] Shirokov, *Textbook of Marxist Philosophy*.
[2] Engels, *Anti-Duhring*.

interposed between receptors and effectors, first to provide a multitude of alternative associations, thus making it possible for the brain to *think* about the situation revealed by the receptors, in order that the effect or discharge may bring about *considered*, problem-solving action. In other words, when matter is organised in nerves it feels and acts, when matter is organised in a human brain *it thinks*. *Thought, mind,* is not a substance added to matter, it is a *function* of a certain kind of matter. This is a conclusion as perfectly in harmony with biological science as mechanistic materialism is in contradiction to it. It is, of course, a view held not only by Marxists but by most, if not all, professional biologists and by an increasing number of philosophers with a real knowledge of biology.

Why Mechanism lapses into Idealism

The mechanistic materialist has formulated his position in an honest endeavour to be true to scientific principles, to seek out scientific causes, to avoid multiplying entities and falling back in every case of difficulty upon the supernatural. He is above all in violent reaction from vitalism, which injects a living force into matter to explain life. He is fundamentally opposed to the theory of the interaction of two completely disparate entities—mind and body.

All this is perfectly correct and, even in this narrow and somewhat rigid form, materialism has broadened the field of science, firmly established the scientific method and done much to overthrow obscurantism and superstition.

But the mechanist in banishing mind from the universe because he cannot accept the interaction of mind and matter, really pre-supposes this fundamental dualism, this parallel existence of a matter without mind and a mind without matter. If he did not have in the back of his head the notion that consciousness is a thing in itself, *that mind could only be* a distinct mind stuff (even though he doesn't believe in it), he would not raise the question as to how interaction is possible. He would not discard consciousness if he did not believe in the first place that consciousness is a mysterious thing which intervenes to make dead matter live. In other words, he himself has an idealistic attitude to the mind. Like the idealist he says : matter cannot think ; and like the idealist he says : if thought exists at all it must exist as a thing in itself, as something mental, out of space and time.

The mechanistic materialist is, in spite of himself, constantly lapsing into idealism. Either he begins to talk about mental end-effects and then finds he has no evidence for the existence of matter at all, or, baffled by having only a physico-chemical universe which is by definition destitute of mind and values, he finds himself driven into supernaturalism. For although *ex hypothesi* matter cannot think and nothing exists except atoms and molecules, it is perfectly clear to the mechanistic materialist in his own experience that the universe contains living, changing, evolving beings, quite unaccountable by the laws of chemistry and physics and quite unpredictable in their developments. Therefore God or the Life Force must breathe into those dead bones the breath of life ; a transcendental world must be superimposed upon the purely physical.

It is the barrenness of mechanism, its complete incapacity to explain the rich, mental, moral and ideal experience of the concrete world that precipitates those who come under its influence into mysticism. Thus a considerable influence in the direction of superstition and mysticism in the world of thought today is mechanistic materialism itself. We shall shortly consider some striking examples, but before doing so it is necessary to find some explanation of this bewildering state of affairs. Why does mechanistic materialism turn into its opposite, idealism ?

CHAPTER IV

WHAT IS MATTER?

Has Matter become Spiritual?

IT is frequently stated today in pseudo-philosophical writings and in the pulpit that the old idea of matter as a non-mental, external and objective reality has gone, that modern science has refined and dissolved matter away into something so intangible, so tenuous, so shot through with purely mental elements as to be, virtually, something more spiritual than material. If this be so, then the idealist's claim is greatly reinforced. There can certainly be a realm of pure spirit, with all that that implies. Endless vistas of spiritual entities open up, none of which, of course, have need to be even associated with a material substratum.

Sir Arthur Eddington and Sir James Jeans did much to popularise such a notion, and it has been taken up enthusiastically by ministers of religion, broadcasters and journalists. Eddington declared that the floor on which we stand is not really solid. " The plank has no solidity of substance. To step on it is like stepping on a swarm of flies."[1] Another writer says, " A table, a piece of paper, no longer possesses *that solid reality which they appear to possess* ; they are both of them porous, and consist of very small electrically charged particles."[2] And Joad pointed out that the materialist view of matter which conceived of " the atom as a hard, simple, obvious little lump of stuff" is out of date. This has disappeared ; modern matter is something infinitely attenuated and elusive. It is a hump in space-time, a " mush of electricity, a wave of probability undulating into nothingness. Frequently it turns out not to be matter at all but a projection from the consciousness of the perceiver."[3]

[1] Eddington, *The Nature of the Physical World.*
[2] Ernest Zimmer, *The Revolution in Physics* (our italics).
[3] Joad, *God and Evil.*

Sir James Jeans summed it up by saying " The fact that so much of what used to be thought to possess an objective physical existence now proves to consist only of subjective mental constructs must surely be counted a pronounced step in the direction of mentalism."[1]

However, Stebbing, who has subjected these philosophical deductions from modern physics to acute criticism in her *Philosophy and the Physicists*, declares, " In my opinion, at least, modern theories of the atom afford not the slightest justification for saying that recent developments in physics have any tendency to show that materialism is false or are capable of being used to provide any argument in favour of idealism."[2]

Three Fallacies

There are three separate fallacies involved in the idealist position here.

Firstly, all that is really meant by modern science is that the nineteenth-century view of matter, at the ultra-microscopic level, is out of date. It no longer consists of hard, indivisible billiard-ball-like atoms but of electrical phenomena. But *neither* view has got anything at all to do with *solidity on the level of ordinary experience*. On that level matter is as solid as ever it was, it not only *appears* to be solid, it *is* solid, it does " possess that solid reality which it appears to possess." The scientist does not deny that however tenuous and impalpable the ultimate constituents of matter may be, the result in our man-size world is ordinary tables and chairs which the scientist believes in like everybody else.

Secondly, however tenuous and non-solid ultra-microscopic matter is found to be, it does not cease to be matter. Matter has merely been further described. It has only ceased to be material in the vulgar use of that word, not in the exact or in the scientific sense. For anything is matter that exists prior to man and prior to mind, that is an objective reality existing independently of the human mind and subsequently known by

[1] Jeans, *Physics and Philosophy*.
[2] Stebbing, *loc. cit.*

it. " The sole property of matter with which materialists are concerned," says Lenin,[1] " is the property of objective reality, of existing outside our cognition. . . . The recognition of immutable elements is not materialism—it is only mechanistic or metaphysical materialism. Do . . . electrons, ether and so on exist as objective realities outside the human mind or not? "[2] When modern science refuted the billard-ball theory of the mechanists, some philosophers " not only threw out the bath water, but the baby as well. By denying the immutability of the elements and properties of matter known hitherto, they ended with the denial of matter, the denial of the objective reality of the physical world."[3]

Thirdly, from the tenuous character of matter on the ultra-microscopic level, from the mathematical abstractions which help us to understand matter at that level, and from the undeniable fact of the relativity of our knowledge (that which we know depends on how we handle it, on our limitations, our conditions of knowledge) they pass over into pure mentalism, as Joad does ; matter becomes " a projection from the consciousness of the perceiver." But this does not follow. We have already discussed the dependence of knowledge on the point of view of the knower and shown that dependence does not rule out independence. The argument is of sufficient importance to be recalled. *That* the object exists independently of us is an unchangeable fact ; *what* it is exactly we know only in part, in aspects, with but an approximate degree of truth. That what we thus know is true as far as it goes we know because we act successfully on that knowledge. So far from matter dissolving into mind, mind remains that which possesses the characteristic of becoming acquainted with things other than itself, while matter remains that which is known. Relativity does not lessen objectivity. All perception is a judgment of *thereness*. We do not *infer* an object because we *have* a perception ; perception involves a judgment of external

[1] Lenin speaks, of course, as a dialectical materialist, not as a mechanist.
[2] Lenin, *Materialism and Empirio-Criticism*.
[3] *Ibid.*

reality and needs no inference. We do not perceive ideas, or abstractions. We perceive *something*.

We thus refute subjectivism not by reasserting a naive, uncritical realism, not by going blindly back to mechanistic materialism, but by taking up into our objectivism the subjective factors of knowledge. We come back to the objective world again but with a new conception of our relation to it, which is no longer that of a contemplative eye passively observing it, or a " spot-light " falling upon it to enable us to " read off " what is *out there*, but is that of an organic unity between knower and known. " Duality in unity is implied in all experience " says James Ward, " but not dualism."

Opening the Door to Superstition

It is doubtful if the views which we have criticised would ever have become so widely held but for the fact that a breach in the walls of scientific knowledge may be expected to let in a host of phantoms from the supernatural realm which may be taken for realities.

If reality is mind, then there may be mental or spiritual realities outside the physical universe, outside of space and time, unknowable and unverifiable by the senses but accessible to spirit through spiritual organs of apprehension or intuition. This belief opens the floodgates to every form of superstition and mentalism.

Instead of seeking out the scientific causes of disease the man who believes in the supernatural may attribute it to black magic, or devils, or a punishment from God. Instead of installing a water-borne sewage system, he resorts to prayer and sacrifice. Natives in Central Africa when they fail in their primitive methods of iron-smelting do not try to find out what technical error they have made, but attribute their failure to someone having bewitched them. Superstition is therefore not only a reflection of ignorance ; it tends to perpetuate it. Eventually science is held to be something blasphemous. It is irreligious to take out of the sphere of the spiritual or of Providence that which rightly belongs to it.

Russian peasants under the Czar attributed famine not to shallow ploughing but to the Divine Wrath. They were taught to accept epidemics as a discipline of the soul. In India today superstition still obstructs social advance. Even in our own country trade depression, wars, disease and poverty are often felt to be divine dispensations, or due to irresistible and inscrutable forces, which it is folly for us to seek to control and presumptuous to seek to understand.

If it should be contrary to the interests of any privileged section of the community to remove these evils, it will be seen how the superstition which paralyses men's efforts serves their ends. In this fact we have, perhaps, one of the reasons for the revival of idealism in an age in which many social evils exist and in which the remedies at hand conflict with vested interests. The approach of scientific reason, in physical science, in biology and medicine, and above all in sociology, is a hard discipline. It is easier to invoke the supernatural or to yield to inscrutable powers, than to wrestle with nature, learn her laws and control the world. In sociology, moreover, the interests of the privileged may be immediately threatened by sound social theory. In that case it will be desirable that knowledge should be clouded and human power to interfere enfeebled.

This does not mean, of course, that every idealist is *consciously* defending his cash interests or the interests of a privileged class, but it does suggest that in a society ruled by and ideologically dominated by such interests there will be a certain pressure or drift away from scientific social thinking and towards idealism, superstition and supernaturalism, and that the greater the danger of social change, the more widespread will superstition tend to become.

There is an implicit irrationalism wherever scientific inquiry is ruled out of any part or experience. All supernaturalism is irrational because in it there can be no discovery of ascertainable and verifiable laws of cause and effect. All is conjecture or dependence on unprovable " revelation ". Men find themselves deducing from unprovable *a priori* principles, as revealed truths, what must or must not be so. The result is that there will be as many systems as there are sets of unproved dogmas, all mutually exclusive. When man cannot find out the truth of science he is forced to accept the truth of his own intuition, and that means complete subjectivism, believing what is strongly, even overwhelmingly, felt to be true at the moment. Psychology tells us what an infinity of mental delusions such beliefs lay us open to.

CHAPTER V

THE RATIONAL ORDER OF NATURE

Natural Law as a Mental Construct

THE attack on the validity of natural science has by no means confined itself to the attempt to use modern theories of matter to rehabilitate supernaturalism. Going back as far as Hume but represented in the nineteenth century by Mach, Avenarius and Karl Pearson, and in more recent years by Poincaré and others, we find a philosophy of science which really cuts the nerve of all scientific knowledge whatsoever.

This is the view that science never gets beyond its own perceptions and the more or less arbitrary ways in which they are built up by the mind into scientific constructs. These come, mistakenly, to be regarded as external objects and scientific laws. "All through the physical world," says Eddington, "runs an unknown content, which must really be the stuff of our own consciousness. We have found that where science has progressed the farthest, the mind has but regained from nature that which the mind has put into nature." Scientific laws and, in fact, the whole scientific description of the world, thus come to be a collection of fictions or abstractions which, to use an example of Eddington's, no more describe the reality they stand for than the numbers of telephone subscribers tell us anything about the subscribers themselves. The theory, in some quarters, is extended to overthrow the whole notion of causation and scientific law and to substitute mere succession or observed regularities. Thus a wire glows when you pass electricity through it, but we must not say that the electricity *causes* the rise in temperature, we have merely two events which frequently occur together so that there is the *probability* of them doing so again. When we heat a metal rod it expands, but there is no reason why we should expect the same result to follow when we heat another rod.   In neither case is there any necessary connection between the so-called cause and effect.

Nor can we say that there is a strong probability that a repetition of the first phenomenon will be followed by the occurrence of the second.   Probability is relative to knowledge.   There is no probability as to the future if we have nothing to go on except the observed succession of events on previous occasions.   Statistics cannot help us unless we have information which takes us beyond these observed events.

Clearly this is a profoundly sceptical view and it is also a denial that nature is a rational order.   By shaking apart the connected parts of organised nature we are left with a meaningless jumble of facts.   Science has ceased to explain anything, it does not penetrate nature's secrets.   All that it does is to summarise observations.   What we call causal laws are ultimately only ways of correlating elements in our experience. This view destroys the picture of the physical world as a causal system in which events are joined together like links in a chain. Without causal laws our observations belong only to the field of history and not to science at all.

Joad rightly says of this attack on causality, " it strikes the authentic subjectivist note."   As Hume argued many years ago, the necessity which seems to bind cause and effect together is really only our subjective *expectation*, there is no real reason why the effect should always follow the cause.   In other words the past does not in fact condition the future.   It is clear that what follows is not merely an end to scientific explanation but to any scientific analysis of the development of society, to all economic theory, and to any philosophy of history.   The world in all its aspects becomes a mere disconnected succession of unrelated facts.

A logical consequence is the denial that such theories as evolution, the planetary hypothesis, the circulation of the blood, the theories explaining the physiological activities of the organism, the existence of molecules, atoms and even cells in any way represent reality.   They are simply logical constructs or frameworks into which observational data can be fitted and which have a certain convenience.

True Explanation Penetrates Nature

This is completely untrue to the real nature of science. An explanatory theory, like any of those mentioned above, achieves logical connection and unification only on the basis of discovering *what lies behind the facts*, for it is this which explains *why* things behave as they do. Now every such scientific explanation invokes elements beyond direct observation, but none the less real on that account. Such elements and explanatory conceptions are not fictions but the most useful and important facts. Around them all investigation turns.

An excellent example is atomic theory. Mach, who took the radical step of *identifying* the physical object with its sensible appearances[1], regarded scientific theories as useful conceptions for summarising and anticipating observations. The atom therefore does not exist, it is a functional idea, abstracted from phenomena, which enables us to handle our data economically. It is a convenient working tool. He thus hoped to get rid of what he called " the metaphysical elements " in science, viz., such entities as atoms, molecules, waves, and such hypotheses as the kinetic theory of heat. But the atom and atomic theory which Mach wished to eliminate have proved to be the turning point of the whole of modern physics. Progress here has not depended on regarding atoms as fictions but upon taking them as real things to investigate. What Mach regarded as speculative and metaphysical we now recognise as the most useful and important facts, around which all investigation turns.

Nor does the advance of science reduce the molecule to a conceptual symbol. Prof. A. R. Todd says, " By means of X-rays we can now take what amount to photographs of the inside of molecules, and these photographs show that molecules really must be very like the models and diagrams that the chemist uses to describe them. They have shape and pattern

[1] Mach, *Analysis of Sensations* (1886) and *Science of Mechanics*.

in space. They are not merely symbols in the mind of the chemist."[1]

I need hardly point out that in the field of human physiology, in which all the important explanatory realities lie definitely *behind* the observational data, there is simply no question that we are describing reality and not using convenient fictions. The blood really does circulate, the processes of digestion and assimilation, the complex and quite invisible excretory mechanism of the kidney, tissue metabolism, etc., are realities, even though far from completely understood. Yet these are typical theories, theories that, like evolution, the planetary hypothesis and the conceptions of atoms and molecules, are now regarded virtually as facts. The law of gravitation, the concept of " plant " and " animal ", the different species of these, are not convenient fictions, inventions of the human intellect, put into nature by us. They are forced upon us by an objective fact that was there before men with the power of conceptual thought existed. Truth is not generated by the mind, it is only grasped by it by way of an infinite process of approximation. It is not a purely mental reality, but a mental picture of reality, of an objective body of fact existing before all knowledge.

What is a Law of Nature ?

It is important to grasp clearly just what an explanatory law is. It is not merely a summary of a number of observations, it gives a view of *what really lies behind those observations* and explains why things happen as they do. It therefore implies the logical deduction of particular facts from more general laws. When we discover such a theory, which links together and explains in this way a number of hitherto unintelligible facts, we do not think of it as a mere formula to cover inexplicable data, we jump at it as a truth, we feel we have penetrated to a deeper level and found something new, that was really there. We have not read the new law into nature, we have read it off.

[1] Professor A. R. Todd, *Molecules and their Structure.*

Perhaps nothing has caused so much confusion or perplexity as the discovery that a very large number of laws have a *statistical* character. This is true, and it might easily be supposed therefore that such laws cannot be more than summaries of unexplained facts.

But let us take an example of such a law. The laws which state how the volume of a gas varies with its temperature are the result of the movement of a very large number of molecules. The laws hold for large numbers. But on the level of the individual molecule the law does not hold at all. Thus the pressure of a gas on a large surface is the same on both sides, but the pressure of a gas on an area one-thousandth of a millimetre square is *not* necessarily the same on both sides.

What does this mean?

It means first of all that the behaviour of the gas molecules in large numbers depends upon the behaviour of the individual molecules, themselves acting according to the laws or modes of behaviour of individuals. The units do not all behave in exactly the same way, yet by reason of how they behave the uniform behaviour of the group is determined. Indeed, the uniformity depends on the non-uniformity, the actual behaviour, the individually different behaviour of the molecules.

This does not even mean that individual reactions are random. They simply have a behaviour *of their own*. But the expectation of the mass behaving according to iron laws which can be depended upon, is based on the fact that there is some determination in the case, even though we do not know enough of what determines the individual event.

The mass law which results is well established and gives us a means of understanding and controlling a huge range of physical phenomena.

In other words even in these statistical regularities we accept causal laws or there would be nothing to depend on. This alone makes science possible, for there is no reason for expecting recurrence unless grounded in the real nature of things.

Thus constancy and variation are polar categories in this case, each implies the other, an excellent example of the interpenetration of opposites.

Nor does the *different* behaviour of molecules taken individually from the effect of all of them taken together mean that lawlessness prevails on the microscopic level. It simply means that the laws here are of a different sort, and that one sort of law on this level results in quite another sort of law on another level, i.e., a law of the way in which multitudes are distributed rather than of the way in which each particle behaves. The result is to confirm rather than to overthrow the generallly accepted laws for gases.

Now when one reaches a real explanation (for instance the theory of evolution as an explanation of the succession of fossil forms, or of the fact that the limbs of such different animals as birds, horses, whales and men are all built on the same basic pattern) one is not merely describing particular facts ; on the contrary, as we have said, one is passing behind the facts to a more general and fundamental truth from which a great variety of facts about fossils, comparative anatomy, embryology and so forth can be logically derived. In other words explanation arranges the individual facts in more general connections, and these are in turn explained, linked together and shown to be necessary by a law of still greater generality. The central notion is that of a system of laws linking and explaining everything. This does not mean, however, that a system of abstract laws or principles determines the facts ; such a notion would be pure idealism. Such a system of laws consists of nothing but the facts themselves seen in greater completeness and interconnectedness, so that explanation still remains within the realm of nature though it penetrates behind the surface phenomena.

Science is eternally committed to the principle that all natural occurrences whatsoever are causally determinate, and therefore scientifically intelligible and explicable. And this is the root not only of science but of human sanity.

Kant well expressed the true scientific integrity which will have no exception to a completely naturalistic explanation of all events, an unbroken chain of cause and effect :—

" I know a not altogether unmanly fear, the fear which shrinks from whatever unsettles reason from her first principles, and opens the door for her to rove through boundless fancies." To admit one single irrationality means that " we are as effectually lost as when we believe a single ghost story or work of magic."[1]

[1] Quoted in Wallace, *Kant*, p. 114.

CHAPTER VI

THE ROOTS OF SANITY

Is Nature a Causal System?

SCIENCE is committed to the principle that all natural existence whatsoever is causally determinate, and therefore scientifically intelligible and explicable. The principle of causation is the root of human sanity.

As is very well known, the philosopher Hume believed that causation could be reduced to the frequent repetition of the sequence of events which we call cause and effect, until whenever we experience the first of these events we *expect* the second. In other words there is no *objective* necessity for the effect to follow, the only necessity is psychological—I find myself believing that it will. Clearly if there is no actual necessity involved, no actual causal connection, then there is no such thing as science, for science is a penetration into the causal network making up the system of nature, not a catalogue of observed associations. Thus if I am deprived of oxygen, I die. Is the certainty merely psychological, because I have got into the *habit* of believing that people will die under such conditions on account of its frequently occurring? Or is there a valid scientific *reason* for death in such a case?

It might be thought that no one in his senses now believes as Hume did. On the contrary, this belief is quite widely accepted. Professor Ayer says, " Our view of the nature of causation remains substantially the same as his."[1] Elsewhere he speaks of " getting rid of the misleading picture of the physical world as a causal system."

If not Science then Faith

Hume thought that reason was not only useless in science but that we " had not the lowest degree of evidence on any proposition either in philosophy or common life." What, then? Are we to do without beliefs? Certainly not, we find

[1] Ayer, *Language Truth and Logic* (Second edition).

53

ourselves continually believing on instinct what cannot be justified by reason, and there is nothing else for us to do, *for we cannot live at all unless we believe*. Therefore Hume makes his sceptical conclusions the very ground for trusting intuition or even authority. So his acute reasoning is used simply to subvert reason. According to Hume, reason cannot assure us of the truths of religion any more than it can vindicate the beliefs of science or even those of common sense. Reason cannot even prove the existence of the body, or support the evidence of the senses. But " since reason is incapable of dispelling these clouds, nature herself suffices to that purpose, and cures me of this philosophical melancholy and delirium ... when after three or four hours' amusement I would return to these speculations, they appear so cold, strained and ridiculous, that I cannot find in my heart to enter into them any farther. Here then I find myself absolutely and necessarily determined to live, and talk, and act like other people in the common affairs of life."[1]

There is a great deal more to this than a cynical attitude to philosophy. It is a powerful intellectual plea for surrendering the intellect in order to put in its place a non-rational faith. This Hume makes plain enough in the last of his *Dialogues Concerning Natural Religion*. Scepticism may destroy one's faith in science, but by doing so it may create faith in the supernatural. For in the first place, since science is not a rational and valid system of truth it cannot disprove religion. And secondly, " A person seasoned with a just sense of the imperfections of natural reason, will fly to revealed truth with the greatest avidity . . . to be a philosophical sceptic is the first and most essential step towards being a sound, believing Christian ", since the failure of reason, *in all fields*, justifies resort to faith both in matters of common sense and in matters of faith.

It may be doubted whether Hume himself really meant this ; but there is no doubt at all that the distrust of reason as an instrument for obtaining knowledge of God is a strong

[1] Hume, *Treatise on Human Nature.*

encouragement to a certain type of mind to find for the beliefs they cannot do without some other sanction than that of critical reason. The reaction, in such cases, is to hark back to traditionalism or to mysticism.

Causation and its Nature

But the empiricist criticism of causation is not merely to be rejected because it is superstitious and anti-scientific. It is useful to examine it, refute it and clarify our minds as to the real nature of scientific reasoning.

In the first place, Hume was criticising a false view of causation which had to be got rid of. Causation had been defined in terms of pure logic, as though the effect were contained in the cause as the conclusion is contained in the premises of a syllogism. Hume rightly points out that this is not so, for if it were we could deduce all possible effects from present knowledge ; but, on the contrary, what effects follow from any cause can only be discovered by observation. In this Hume was perfectly right. The empiricist is right as against the " nature philosophy " which is prepared to discover all scientific truth by pure deduction from first principles[1] (or even from what we know empirically already).

Secondly, we tend to see in cause and effect a kind of " push " in the cause which passes over into the effect, as when one billiard ball hits another ; or it may be that we reason from the analogy of the will ; I *will* to raise my arm, and I do, is not cause and effect something like that ? But there is no *force* making things happen, and here again Hume is right.

Thirdly, if no effect can be simply *deduced* from the cause, there is something unpredictable *in the first instance* in the effect. In other words, prior to observation we do not know what effects will follow from a given cause, for example that a given wave-length produces as an effect the sensation of red. To find out we must try the experiment and observe the result.

But are we to conclude from this that we can do nothing but put on record that A is always followed by B ?

[1] E.g. Schelling.

On the contrary, science is never content with a merely descriptive account of what happens when a given cause is operating. Of course, very often we cannot get beyond the empirical fact, but that is always regarded as unsatisfactory and as the posing of an unanswered question to science, and *not* as a scientific result. As an example we may mention the effect of certain drugs, such as digitalis ; it *has* a certain effect, but we don't know why. In other cases we do know why, or we know some of the why ; that is the beginning of a scientific account of causation. In other words, causation is not the bare fact of B following A, it is the discovery of what is responsible for this effect. Now only on this level do we come to feel that the effect does not merely happen, but *has* to happen.

It is unscientific, not the last word in science, as Ayer and his fellow positivists believe, to accept a bare factual succession ; pollen from grass gives me hay fever ; I want to know *why* ? Science looks for causal relationships in nature which are responsible for empirical sequences ; it passes over to *explanation*. Thus I feel a bit happier about an illness if my doctor can tell me *why* I am feeling run down, or *why* I have proved susceptible to a certain infection. The more he knows apart from *the immediate occasion* of the illness the more likely he is to be able to help me.

Causation and the Antecedent Conditions

This gives us the clue to a more scientific account of causation. Hume and the man in the street tend to regard as *the cause* of an event just *one* factor. In point of fact it is a large group of antecedent conditions, some of which we usually ignore. Thus if a house catches fire it may be attributed to a match being thrown into a waste-paper basket ; but really we should add the inflammable material inside the basket, and then, outside, the presence of oxygen in the air, the absence of someone in the room who could have noticed it, the carelessness of the smoker, the type of matches he used, and so on. In cases of illness, for example, what we call pre-disposing causes are as important as the immediate occasion of the disease.

This brings us much closer to the real nature of causality. The cause is the whole assemblage of conditions which, when all are present, has a certain result. That it has such a result can only be known after the event, but thereafter we may consider it as an established regularity which we can depend on. It is of the nature of a general law. Such a regularity is first formulated as a hypothesis (not as an induction from one or two cases, but as a hypothesis *suggested* by one, or two, cases). It may subsequently either be verified by proving dependable in practice, or itself *explained* as one case of a more general law. Thus the snapping of a crankshaft may be an example of metal fatigue.

It must be realised that any set of conditions which always gives a certain result, e.g. the filament in a bulb beginning to glow, always leaves us with a further problem on our hand, with other causal relations to enquire into. Thus I may be satisfied for the moment that resistance to an electric current results in incandescence : so far the glowing filament is explained ; but if I am possessed by insatiable curiosity I shall soon be asking more questions, requiring further explanations on a deeper level. However, the fact that further explanations are possible does not invalidate the relatively satisfactory explanation given when I go beyond the bare fact of " it is the electric current " to a fuller explanation, bringing in the heat generated by resistance, the vacuum or gas in the bulb and so on. In fact, in many cases this sort of thing will legitimately be regarded as a genuine scientific explanation— all that is wanted at the moment.

Nature and the Contingent

We may now add that explanatory regularities which are then comprehended under wider generalisations, and these in their turn under wider theories still, help to build up our knowledge of the structure of reality as an interlocking causal system. The fact that it is far from complete does not render the achievement any less important and significant.

Now this has already taken the simple A followed by B

sequence far beyond the mere empirical regularity and the psychological expectation generated by it. The effect is to reduce the contingency—contingency being the bare, arbitrary, inexplicable *fact* that A *is* always followed by B. Hume, Ayer and the rest stop there. We have gone far beyond it. We have not *eliminated* contingency, within our explanation there are still some ultimate because *at present* inexplicable facts, but we have *reduced* it, and we have knit the isolated causal sequence into a system by showing that it is one case of a wider law (even though that law is itself at present only empirically established). Thus if I explain several examples of illness as due to vitamin deficiency, then, even if I am still not sure exactly why Vitamin A does this and Vitamin B prevents that, each illness is no longer seen as just happening. On the contrary, given knowledge of the properties of vitamins and of the symptoms resulting from their deficiency the symptoms follow logically and are in that sense necessary or inevitable. Of course, the fact that a particular vitamin is necessary for proper bone formation may still be contingent[1] (and even if we find out why, there will still be some contingency behind that), but even so the discovery of vitamins and the results of their deficiency has considerably diminished contingency.

An important conclusion follows. While *some* power over nature follows from *any* generalisation however simple (e.g. hot air rises, ice floats), *far more* control over nature follows when we push the contingency further back by bringing the simple regularities under a wider law, say the gas laws in general. The greater measure of control is a result of building our knowledge of the structure of nature, grasping a systematic account of it. There is a foolish perfectionism which wants all or nothing, which is so dissatisfied with any remaining contingency as to consider the partial system not worth having. Such persons do not usually refuse to take advantage of the innumerable benefits which flow from systematic science in medicine, in engineering, in chemistry, in electricity, and

[1] By *contingent*, one means that the facts *are* just so, we don't know why.

yet it is surely in this really tremendous control over nature
that the vindication of causality is found.

Mere empiricism would never reach even the beginnings of
science (for science is always a first step in *explanation* and thus
in *system making* and not a mere recording of an invariable
sequence). Had its view prevailed there would be no science,
but only the empiricism of herbal remedies and rule-of-thumb
techniques. *They* would not take us very far.

The Fear of finding too much

In so far as merely empirical theories are accepted today
they hamper science, hold us back from discovering wider
laws and theories. They would seem to bear witness to a
certain fear of finding out too much.

Professor Stebbing, in her devastating analysis of irrationalism among the physicists, says : " It is odd to find that the
view that ' all is mysterious ' is to be regarded as a sign of
hope, odd that we should congratulate ourselves that *we* put
into Nature the laws we profess to discover, that men should
have come to this pass—that they welcome any indication of
unreason in the world."[1]

But is it so strange ? The attitude of the modern world to
science changed when its civilisation started to show signs of
age and decay. It became day by day more obvious that it
could not solve the problems created by its own industrial
revolution ; that its economics of abundance turned into an
economics of poverty leading to wars and depressions ; that
its expanding democracy turned into restrictive plutocracy ;
that production for the profit of the employers is a suicidal
way of running the human household, leading to unemploy-
ment and starvation. Even technological progress turned
from friend to foe. New inventions were feared, they were
bought in order to be suppressed. Science, the former ally
and auxiliary force, became an enemy of the existing social
order. Bourgeois civilisation can no longer cope with its own
problems, therefore man and nature, human society and

[1] Stebbing, *Philosophy and the Physicists.*

economics, must appear incalculable. If reason reigns, then bourgeois civilisation has to admit its own impotence and bankruptcy ; hence reason must be dethroned.

The greatest fear is lest causal law be applied to society and to history. Even where its validity is accepted in the physical world it is denied in relation to human affairs ; but the safest course is to have no truck with it at all.

Of course, we cannot solve human problems with laws appropriate only to physics. Who wants to ? The problems may be, indeed are, more complex and difficult, but they are no more difficult than chemistry appeared when we first began to study it. It is not so much the difficulty that daunts as the fact that " those especially who cherish specific forms of institutional life—economic, familial, religious, educational— are loath to allow the truth of any discoveries whose consequences are opposed to their special interests ".[1]

Perhaps this gives us the real clue to the cult of un-reason which is so prevalent today, which glories in the notion that the foundations of the world were laid amid impenetrable fog, as a contemporary philosopher neatly puts it.

We have been warned that in an advanced civilisation like our own " the absence of a co-ordinating philosophy of life, spread throughout the community, spells decadence, boredom and the slackening of effort ",[2] and that no technology or scientific methodology, no belief in natural law and no intelligent purpose in organised human life is possible unless we believe in some measure of regularity, persistence and recurrence in nature based on an ordered structure which lies open in every detail to human understanding.

[1] Edel, *The Theory and Practice of Philosophy.*
[2] Whitehead, *Adventures of Ideas.*

CHAPTER VII

THE NATURE OF THE SUPERNATURAL

Does Science exclude the Supernatural?

THE upshot of all those theories that confuse modern ideas of matter with the reduction of the material to something mental, as of all forms of vitalism, is to demonstrate one thing at least, that science does not *exclude* the possibility of the supernatural. At any point, that is to say, the natural order may be interrupted by phenomena only explicable in terms of a transcendental reality. The significance of such an attitude of mind is immense. To look everywhere for the supernatural suspends those processes of intellectual liberation by which " men are brought to sanity "[1] and begin to understand the science of society. If whenever we meet with something we cannot yet explain scientifically we immediately regard it as beyond a natural explanation there is little incentive for further investigation. But if science comes to a full stop, so does human progress. A hundred years ago nature was full of unexplained phenomena that are now understood. The faith of science was that they were problems for rational solution, and that faith has been vindicated. Had such phenomena been regarded as examples of Divine intervention not one of these discoveries would have been made. The object of science is to give a natural, rational account of things, not to invoke inscrutable powers to explain them away. It is not fair to insist on a natural explanation for easy things and for all past discoveries which are now generally accepted and to fall back on supernaturalism for the difficult ones. If we bring in supernatural agencies at one point we may as well bring them in at all points and save ourselves the trouble of constructing a trivial man-made rational order.

" Faith in the Supernatural ", says Santayana, " is **a**

[1] Laski, *Faith, Reason and Civilisation.*

61

desperate wager made by man at the lowest ebb of his fortunes; it is as far as possible from being the source of that normal vitality which subsequently, if his fortunes mend, he may gradually recover."[1]

He is right. If man's earlier belief in the supernatural derived from his ignorance and helplessness in the face of a nature hardly understood at all and almost completely man's master, belief in the supernatural today arises from the failure of nerve in Western civilisation in the period of capitalist decline. The same force which drove the ancient world into the shelters of pagan and Christian supernaturalism drives us into a similar flight from responsibility, both on the plane of action and on the plane of belief.

Man will not be delivered from superstition by the most overwhelming case for reason if a deep reluctance based on a conscious or unconscious fear of what enquiry may reveal if science is applied to the objective social situation holds him back. When reason and scientific enquiry conflict with the *status quo* the tendency is to scrap them both.

Supernaturalism and Social Chaos

In this whole degeneration into supernaturalism and irrationalism we have quite clearly the story of an outworn élite which could always find the word to justify its fatigue and excuse its panic fear.

To those who are shut up in the capitalist world and are unable or unwilling to conceive of its ending in order to give place to socialism, it can only seem that the world is going mad. Alexander Miller, a Christian who is deeply troubled by the course of events, describes the predicament thus :

" Events are out of hand, our generation is in the grip of gigantic forces whose nature no man can understand and which are beyond the power of men or of democratic assemblies to control. The future of society is being shaped by influences impersonal or daemonic so that intelligent intervention is impossible or meaningless. This sense of overmastering fate

[1] Santayana, *The Realm of Spirit.*

is shattering in its effect on personal responsibility. It takes the stuffing out of men ; it creates a numbness of mind and soul, a sense of helpless and sheer frustration."[1]

The B.B.C. and the Reconciliation of Faith and Science

In the Autumn of 1952 a number of working scientists gave a series of broadcasts on *Science and Faith*,[2] introduced and finally summed up by Professor John Baillie. None of these men would for a moment tolerate the suggestion of a super-natural intervention breaking in on a chemical or electrical or biological experiment, but they all advocated a fundamental dualism in life, dividing it into the sphere of scientific truth and the sphere of spiritual reality. There is the impersonal, purely mechanical world of science, which is concerned with the " how of things ", with devising means, and there is the personal, spiritual world of religion, which is concerned with the " why " of life, the meaning and purpose of existence, with the choice therefore of ends and with values.

These two worlds are complementary, though how they are to be related, says Baillie, remains a difficult problem.

Science cannot do without faith because of itself it has no values, no aims and no significance. " Science does not possess in itself the necessary nourishment of its own vitality . . . When nature is believed to have no pre-ordained meaning or purpose in itself, speculative interest in it fails, and the remaining concern is only to subdue its inherent purposeless-ness to our own chosen ends." But if such ends are " merely chosen and not prescribed, if they represent only human preference dictated by interest instead of solemn obligations emanating from a source beyond ourselves, then science becomes a dangerous tool to put into men's hands ". Indeed if man's destiny is to control nature, *it is* " *to be controlled by obedience to divinely ordained laws without consideration of convenience, or comfort, or material gain or even survival* "[3] (our italics).

[1] Alexander Miller, *The Christian Significance of Karl Marx.*
[2] Since published as *Science and Faith* edited by Prof. John Baillie.
[3] Prof. John Baillie in *Science and Faith.*

Science by itself can only give us bigger bombs and deeper dug-outs, more power and more comfort. It cannot supply moral resources or good will, faith or hope or charity. " The only certainties for which you and I would lay down our lives are certainties that science can do nothing either to suggest or establish."[1] Science, says John Baillie, is not only incapable of recognising values, it is essentially a dehumanising force, destroying faith in ideals and freedom. The moment you begin to think in terms of values, ends, purposes and human freedom you have left the world of science behind, for science is mechanical, determinist and concerned only with the measurable aspects of phenomena—and what are those but the mere shadows of realities?

Quite other faculties than those we use in scientific investigation put us in contact with the wider world outside that of matter and the measurable, give us intuitive knowledge of a Divine person, acquaint us with religious truths and enable us to recognise the good. Dr. Kenneth Walker believes that these special faculties can be trained to apprehend knowledge directly and not through the senses and the intellect. They give us the knowledge that behind outward appearances there is a supreme spiritual reality.[2]

Literature and Supernaturalism

A somewhat similar approach has been made by a number of literary figures, among whom we may mention T. S. Eliot, Basil Willey, C. S. Lewis and Dorothy Sayers. They assert that in the seventeenth century, with the rise of physical science, there occurred a split between intellect and feeling. From science arose a liberal humanism that undermined poetry and religion, so that man chose a humanistic instead of a theological world view. From this defeat of religion and feeling all our present ills derive—the crisis in morals, the decline of faith, social collapse, the disintegration of culture.

[1] *Ibid.*
[2] Kenneth Walker, *Meaning and Purpose.*

This is why our moral progress has not kept pace with scientific and material advance.

A similar disparagement of science is also found among those who believe in original sin as the cause of all human ills, the consequence of this belief being the surrender of the sociological and psychological approach to abnormalities in human conduct, since the real cause of wrong doing is revealed in theology and not to science.

The way to truth, then, is to turn our backs on reason and science and seek another pathway to reality. This is the two truths theory as expounded and criticised by Kathleen Nott.[1] Having first of all strictly limited science to the quantitative and to the physical, and the scientific reason to the process of analysing facts or taking them to pieces, it is perfectly easy to show that science is inadequate as a method of apprehending moral, aesthetic and human values. The argument proceeds to claim that since by such an emasculated kind of reasoning we cannot know the truth about man, therefore we can know the truth about God by some other means, in this case by the acceptance of authoritarian dogma. "When science is merely measurement, ignorance can be not only bliss, but knowledge."[2] We are thus enabled to return to dogmatic positions which are, of course, unsupported by experimental evidence and reason.

Is Science purely Quantitative ?

It is not difficult to see the fallacies in this reasoning.

1. Reason is not necessarily physical or mathematical or analytical. It is the impartial examination of experimental data, the drawing of inferences therefrom and checking these by further experience.

2. So far from being purely analytical, reason is imaginative and creative, but it continues to test the hypotheses resulting from creative thinking in order to check their validity.

3. Science covers a much wider field than the quantitative

---

[1] Kathleen Nott, *The Emperor's Clothes.*
[2] *Ibid.*

and is by no means confined to mathematical prediction ; if it were, this would automatically exclude the social and non-quantitative biological sciences from scientific status. In point of fact whenever we are able to observe facts and to form hypotheses which we can subsequently test we are thinking scientifically, whatever the subject matter. Why then, is science so frequently stated to be a purely quantitative affair ? The limitation of science to the quantitative is not an accident nor is it wholly due to ignorance. It has the effect of keeping all vital and human and social phenomena out of the field of scientific thinking and therefore handing them over to intuition on the one hand or dogma on the other. It is a shocking argument, because " even if science did not tell us anything about certain fields, not to know something does not mean the same as to know something quite different ",[1] It is clear that Eliot, Willey and the rest have created a fictitious, abstract sort of science and scientist, the bogy which reduces the universe to dead soulless mechanism and is of course indispensable to them when they proceed to show us their alternative road to truth.

4. So far from scientific method being limited, it is the only method by which we get knowledge. We know in one way, not two, and the knowledge we obtain does not fall into two irreconcilable sectors but is always being unified, being built up into one system of truth. It is thinking of this sort that gives us not only modern techniques and modern medicine, but sane political thinking, anthropology, psychology and every other science of man. And every step takes us away from authoritarianism, religious dogma and belief in original sin. " It is not science that is to blame for our troubles but the failure to think scientifically over a wider field and in a more thorough fashion."[2]

5. The argument for two truths is indeed thoroughly suspect. To keep the human and social fields out of the sphere of scientific enquiry is not merely obscurantist, it serves

[1] Kathleen Nott, *loc. cit.*
[2] *Ibid.*

definite social interests. It clearly aims at a return to ecclesiastical authority which is in alliance with corrupt and power-seeking reactionary forces. So far from science being without standards and humanism being without values and aims, it is the churchmen who are continually coming forward in support of atomic bombing and who had nothing to say at the horror of Hiroshima. It has been pointed out that historically war has been nearer to " total " the more religious it has been. Nor are we too happy about the order and values which, according to Eliot, religion is to help us establish ; he would appear to mean the order of an imposed Catholic dogma and the hierarchical, caste system of society it supports, while his values are those of an economically privileged class.

We see that the whole position both of the broadcasters and the literary propagandists derives its strength from a misrepresentation of the nature of science and of modern materialism. It may have been true that some nineteenth-century materialists advanced an over-simplified doctrine which explained away all human values ; but it is not easy to find examples, and there are no such materialists today.

" Nothing But " Philosophies

Those who seek in this way to restore supernaturalism identify scientific materialism with a crude philosophy which " reduces " all the richness of existence to " nothing but " atoms in motion, everything else being mere illusion or a secondary product of no ultimate reality ; they then employ this identification to charge materialists with the reduction of all distinctively human values, moral, aesthetic and so forth, to blind mechanical conjunctions of material entities—a reduction which is in effect the complete destruction of these values.

In point of fact modern, dialectical materialism stands in fundamental opposition not only to all forms of super-naturalism, but also to all types of reductionist thinking of the " nothing but " type. The richness and variety of natural phenomena and human experience cannot be explained away and " reduced " to something else. The world is not really " nothing but ", something other than it appears to be ; it is what it is, in all its manifold variety, with all its distinctive kinds of activity. Human life in particular displays characteristic ways of action which have no counterpart in the behaviour of other living things. Man's intelligence, his problems of technical mastery of the world and social organisation for production, his moral responsibility, his ideal enterprises of art, science and philosophy, are what they are, and are not reducible to anything else.

We thus advance against supernaturalism a materialism at once anti-dualist and anti-reductionist, extending the scope of the natural to include " the whole of man's physical and terrestial environment, earth and sky, land and sea, plants and animals, everything from the structure of the atom to the composition of the galaxy, and from the non-filterable virus to the saints and sages of mankind ".[1]

Science Truly Human

Science itself is thus truly human. " Giving a real understanding of life and therefore also of man, showing man the right way to think in order to understand nature and life, including himself, science can thus provide the basis for a single comprehensive system of thought covering the organic as well as the inorganic world, and therefore relevant to man himself ".[2] Man cannot be dealt with scientifically except on his own level as a member of society, and therefore science itself (not some instrument of knowledge proceeding on non-scientific lines) must be extended to include economics, sociology and psychology.

When that is not done man is treated either mechanically or merely biologically on the one hand, or mystically and in isolation from nature on the other. The latter course must lead straight to superstition and pessimism, as it manifestly has done in the recent broadcasts. Even Canon Raven characterises

[1] Raven, *Science and Religion.*
[2] *loc. cit.*

this dualism as opening the door to superstition. When religion is put into a category by itself to control and guide science from without, by applying supernatural standards, the resulting dualism leads to scepticism, defeatism and subjectivism. There can be no criterion as to objectivity or reliability, or any possibility of distinguishing between good and bad institutions, true insights and pure self-delusion.

The Perils of Subjectivism

Mystical experiences and bad philosophy are poor props for a transcendental faith. Modern psychology offers no support for contact with the supernatural in mystical experiences, which can be shown to be wholly subjective and can be brought about by a considerable range of drugs.[1]

In this welter of subjectivism there can and does arise a conflict of the most dangerous kind ; for supernatural illumination is claimed for opposing convictions, and since rational and scientific criteria have been abandoned one intuition is as good as another. The result is the most fundamental kind of discord that can possibly exist, the only escape being a desperate appeal to some supernatural authority to guarantee one set of revealed truths as against its rivals. It becomes a case of Pope versus the Bible (as interpreted by someone of course), or of prophet versus priest, or mystic versus mystic.

Such a faith, therefore, unless it reverts to authoritarianism, becomes a faith in the divine authority of one's own spiritual insight. But as G. K. Chesterton once said : " Of all horrible religions the most horrible is the worship of the god within . . . That Jones shall worship the god within turns out ultimately to mean that Jones shall worship Jones. Let Jones worship the sun or moon, anything rather than the inner light ; let Jones worship cats or crocodiles, if he can find any in his street, but not the god within ".[2]

[1] See for instance the mystical states self-induced by William James by means of nitrous oxide, as described in *The Will to Believe*.

[2] G. K. Chesterton, *Orthodoxy*.

Supernaturalism blocks progress

Belief in the supernatural is in any scientist a betrayal of the scientific attitude. As long ago as 460 B.C. Hippocrates pointed the way to the emancipation of science from super-stition. Primitive people were irresistibly tempted to consider disease as a supernatural infliction. Insanity or epidemics seem direct visitations from heaven. The Jews of Christ's era regarded epileptics as " possessed with a devil " and the fifth-century Greeks called that mysterious complaint " the sacred illness ". Hippocrates firmly rejected such ideas, and laid down the momentous principle that all disease is natural in origin, and to be cured, not by magic or incantation, but by natural means. " This disease ", he said of epilepsy, " seems to me no more divine than the rest ; but it is as natural as all other diseases and has a cause for all its symptoms." He goes on to say that to know the cause is to know the cure and finally repudiates the distinction between the natural and the supernatural.

The consequences likely to flow from a reversion to super-naturalism would be disastrous. Firstly, it puts a heavy discount upon resources potentially available for the better-ment of human life. Let us remember that one of the most serious of its doctrines is a low view of human capacities, so low in fact that reliance upon them can only make things worse. Science cannot help ; industry and commerce cannot help ; political reform cannot help ; human morals and will power cannot help. The effect of this pessimism can only be that human effort is weakened and frustrated in just the degree in which supernaturalism prevails.

If science represents only the material and inferior aspect of things while another sort of knowledge reveals a higher realm of truth, is it possible in this atmosphere for science to advance to its full stature and accomplish all that it is capable of ? Denial of full scope and responsibility to science on the grounds that its inferior field of work incapacitates it from exercising any positive influence in human affairs can only restrict and deflect its influence.

This opinion of science tends to lower the intellectual standards of supernaturalists in the field of science, to dull their sense of the importance of evidence, to blunt their sensitivity to the need of accuracy of statement and to encourage a resort to feelings and intuitions instead of rational thinking.

Supernaturalism and Dogmatism

What must be the effect of believing that there stands above the enquiring, patient, ever learning and tentative methods of science an organ or faculty which reveals ultimate and immutable truths and that apart from the truths thus obtained there is no sure foundation for morals or for a moral order of society ?

Firstly, it leads to finalism and dogmatism, even to fanaticism.

Secondly, as we have already pointed out, the clash of intuitively perceived or dogmatically advanced absolutes demands an external authority to make known these truths and set the seal on those which are to be believed in distinction from those that are to be rejected.

Thirdly, once an absolute truth or morality is advanced it is lifted above the possibility of criticism because the absolute is the isolated and the isolated is that which cannot be judged on the grounds of connections that can be investigated. Every class interest in all history has defended itself from examination by putting forth claims to absoluteness, taking refuge in the fortress of principles too absolute to be subjects of doubt and inquiry. The real reason that absolutism advances its claims against the verifiable and experimental results of the " lower " methods of science is simply that the search for connections of events, which they deprecate, is the sure way of destroying the privileged position of exemption from inquiry which every form of absolutism secures wherever it obtains.

CHAPTER VIII

WITCHCRAFT AND THE PROFESSORS

1. Professor Polanyi and the Magicians

THE close connection of contemporary philosophy of science with class interests has been strikingly revealed in a series of broadcasts and articles by Professor Michael Polanyi. It is sometimes as valuable to read bad philosophy as good. Good philosophy may tell us the truth about the universe, but bad philosophy may tell us something of the mind of man. It may not tell us the truth about the universe, but it cannot fail to tell us the truth about its author. It does much more than that, it tells us the truth about its readers. Even writing as dishonest intellectually as Polanyi's is startlingly honest as a public document.

He begins by telling us[1] that the Azande in the Southern Sudan have a system of magical beliefs which cunningly allows for every apparent failure in experience. The blindness of the Azande to facts which to us seem decisive is sustained by remarkable ingenuity. " They reason excellently " (says Evans-Pritchard) " in the idiom of their beliefs, but they cannot reason outside, or against, their beliefs because they have no other idiom in which to express their thoughts." Polanyi proceeds to point out that almost any system of beliefs, scientific or otherwise, even one as erroneous as the Ptolemaic theory of the solar system, can be sustained in the face of any number of evidential discrepancies by the simple process of multiplying subordinate hypotheses. By accounting for motions of the planets, which a simple system of circular orbits with the earth as centre could not explain, by making them move in smaller circular orbits on the existing orbit, and then postulating still other smaller orbits on these, the

[1] *The British Journal for the Philosophy of Science*, Vol. III, No. 11 Article, " The Stability of Beliefs ", by Michael Polanyi.

Ptolemaic system accounted with a fair degree of accuracy for the apparent motions of the heavenly bodies as seen from the earth, assumed to be fixed in the centre of the universe. It was completely wrong but it lasted for 1,400 years. " It is impossible " says Polanyi, " to overthrow a theory by advancing facts which are inconsistent with it. Supplementary—'epicyclic' —hypotheses can always be advanced to extend the original theory to cover the new facts ".[1] Circularity in the argument is involved, since the theory is always *assumed* to be true, so that explanations *must* be found. But granted a readily available reserve of epicyclic elaborations and the consequent suppression in the germ of any rival cónceptual development, we may achieve a remarkable degree of stability for almost any system of beliefs. Professor Ayer lends support to Polanyi when he says, " It is nearly always possible to save a theory if you are prepared to make enough additional hypotheses ". Now Polanyi proceeds to argue that science itself is such a system. It is a faith, it is the acceptance of a tradition. To be a scientist one must become a member of the tribe with its whole outfit of traditional beliefs, pre-suppositions, unchallengeable first principles. Science, he argues, is not self-justifying. It can only be accepted in a spirit of uncritical detachment.

But if so, is not religion in precisely the same situation ? It too is a water-tight system of beliefs with supplementary theories for every possible difficulty—the existence of pain and sin, the apparent lack of Divine control in history. Whether you believe in science, or witchcraft, or Christianity, or the principles of the Conservative Party, you must join a "Church" with its unproveable, dogmatic creed. You are simply a believer. Here, Polanyi argues, we have the sanction for " abandoning the critical obsession " and acquiring the capacity to hold beliefs.

It is amazing to find a competent scientist making such complete nonsense of his own profession. Professor Polanyi

[1] The orthodox theory of genetics can be maintained in the same way in spite of mounting evidence to the contrary, as Professor Waddington has recently explained.

surely believes that the Ptolemaic astronomy has been refuted and is not merely discarded as lacking the neatness of the Copernican theory. I am quite certain that he believes in oxygen as a gas and in the process of oxidation and not in the exploded " phlogiston " theory. He does not accept the circulation of the blood on faith, he knows that it is a fact. He knows that the major theories of his own science, chemistry, give a view of what really lies behind experience and thus explain why things behave as they do. But Polanyi is prepared to subvert his own science in order to rehabilitate religion, even if in order to do so he must drag science back into the crudest obscurantism.

How intellectual integrity is thus subverted by the " will to believe " becomes clear when he confesses explicitly just what his motive is in arguing in this way. " Fundamental beliefs ", he says, " spring from the political will, the will to accept, sustain and support the type of society which is felt to be in danger." This " will to believe " produces the beliefs necessary to uphold such a society. We must recognise " the connection between the kind of society we want and the kind of beliefs we have to hold in order that society may be able to exist ".

And yet Marxists are reproached for pointing out that ideologies are created to defend the interests of social classes, and are not the result of a disinterested search for truth !

This whole conception of " belief " is, of course, pragmatic. The very conception of objective truth has gone. These people do not really believe. They only believe that they have the right to believe what they believe. It is necessary for us to hold such systems of belief, they say. The validity of belief, lies in their continuing to work. There is an authoritative need to believe the things that are necessary to the human mind. But surely one of those necessities is precisely a belief in objective truth. Pragmatism is a matter of human needs ; and one of the first of human needs is to be something more than a pragmatist.

2. Professor Broad and Psychical Research

A great deal of light is thrown on contemporary philosophy as we find it in the analytical or positivist school of Moore, Broad, Russel and Ayer by the attitude of Professor Broad to psychical research.[1]

Broad enunciates certain basic principles, mostly of a negative or restrictive kind, which lay down the limits of material phenomena. E.g. *1*, A body cannot enter or leave a closed vessel as long as the walls are intact. *2*, The weight of an object at the earth's surface cannot be altered except by immersing it in fluids of various densities. *3*, A human mind cannot *directly* initiate or modify the motion of any material thing except certain parts of its own organism, such as its arms and legs, and so on. He then proceeds to say that if anything really contradicts these principles, and does not merely appear to do so, we are confronted with the miraculous. Broad regards telepathy and certain other " paranormal " phenomena as well attested, and finds in this breach of his basic principles evidence of the supernatural and therefore of the possibility of human survival after death.

He proceeds to advance the hypothesis of a psychic factor acting along with but independently of the brain. There is nothing against it " except a superstitious objection to dualism " ; and it leaves open the possibility " that these debatable phenomena are genuine." In that case the brain is not an organ productive of thoughts, for it is the psychic factor that thinks and is capable of remembering everything. The brain acts as a kind of sieve ; its function is elimination ; it keeps us from being overwhelmed and confused by irrelevant knowledge.

Broad finds here a slender foothold for the re-establishment of religion. " Ordinary human nature abhors a vacuum, and it will not for long rest content without some system of emotionally toned and unverifiable apocalyptic beliefs for which it can live and die and persecute and endure. When I contemplate communism and fascism, the two new religions. . . .

[1] Broad, *The Mind and its Place in Nature* and *Religion, Philosophy and Psychical Research.*

I appreciate the concluding lines of Mr. Belloc's *Cautionary Tale* about the boy who ran away from his nurse in the zoo and was eaten by a lion. 'Always keep a-hold of Nurse, for fear of finding Something Worse'."

If by chance any misguided seeker after religious consolation should grasp at Broad's outstretched hand he might be advised to ask himself whether the case for religion is really helped by arguments of this kind. If the philosophy of Plato, the arguments of scholastic theologians, the mystical ecstasies of Juliana of Norwich, the meditations of Traherne and the metaphysical speculations of theistic philosophers need to be verified by the predictions of American undergraduates in the matter of the fall of a card or of dice, then religion must indeed be in a very poor way. Such levity lies beyond any useful comment. If any such seeker should grasp such proferred help he would find himself in the position of those who thought that quantum physics helped with the problem of freedom of the will—out on a limb. Professor A. E. Heath rightly says of such thinking, " I have an uneasy suspicion that a great deal of the contemporary interest in these things comes from undercurrents of human feeling and not from objective concern with unusual statistical results."[1]

Professor Broad reveals an amazing blindness to science. Would not any honest investigator say of data which did not fit into his " basic limiting principles " either that the data were wrong, as has often enough been the case, or statistically inaccurate as to their correlation, or else that subsequent developments of science itself will account for them ? Radio, X-rays, vitamins, hormones, bacteria and a thousand phenomena once inconceivable and totally inexplicable are now comprehended within the orbit of natural science, yet they could all have been attributed quite easily to the supernatural.

If the negative and restricting principles of former days, which might well have included action at a distance, the impenetrability of opaque surfaces to rays and so on, had been

[1] Professor A. E. Heath in *The Rationalist Annual*, 1948.

invoked rather than altered, then wireless sets would be evidences of the supernatural and a gateway to paradise.

Any scientist could knock Broad's restrictive principles to pieces in five minutes ; and if further principles were formulated could they be anything more than milestones in the advance of science to ever new frontiers ?

Still more amazing is Broad's conception of the brain as an eliminative organ behind which lies a non-material thinking substance. The dependence of thoughts on the brain is so completely established and so well substantiated by neurological research that any denial of it simply rules the objector out as hopelessly ignorant of modern science.

We are back at the outworn dualism of Descartes (only something even more preposterous, for Descartes would never have made the brain an instrument of thinking) which has been described by Professor Gilbert Ryle as the myth of " the ghost in the machine." " There is thus a polar opposition between mind and matter, an opposition which is often brought out as follows. Material objects are situated in a common field, known as ' space ', and what happens to one body in one part of space is mechanically connected with what happens to other bodies in other parts of space. But mental happenings occur in insulated fields, known as ' minds ', and there is, apart maybe from telepathy, no direct causal connection between what happens in one mind and what happens in another. Only through the medium of the public physical world can the mind of one person make a difference to the mind of another. The mind is its own place and in his inner life each of us lives the life of a ghostly Robinson Crusoe. People can see, hear and jolt one another's bodies, but they are irremediably blind and deaf to the workings of one another's minds and inoperative upon them.

" Such in outline is the official theory. I shall often speak of it, with deliberate abusiveness, as ' the dogma of the Ghost in the Machine '. I hope to prove that it is entirely false, and false not in detail but in principle."[1]

[1] Gilbert Ryle, *The Concept of Mind.*

Broad's dualism has led him, on the one hand, to speculations on spiritualism and on the other to a complete failure
to apply scientific thought rigorously to the world and society.
Broad as a logician is more interested in discussing the
meaning of a sentence than whether it correctly represents
objective reality. Like the whole tribe of contemporary
British philosophers, he has abandoned the search for what he
does not know and concentrated his attention on finding out
the meaning of sentences dealing with what he knows already.
This has the advantage of leading to great precision in the use
of language, but the disadvantage of ceasing to find anything
to say. When philosophers have nothing to say they talk
about language. The consequence of this is that the real
world is left unexamined and uncriticised, in which case
the philosopher may well betray an incredible naiveté about
contemporary life or simply echo the typical clichés and con-
ventional judgments of his class. On the other hand, he may
feel emboldened to speculate about those problems on which
critical thought has nothing to say. This may lead him to a
crude belief in " the Ghost in the Machine" and ultimately
to still cruder beliefs about ghosts.

This becomes abundantly plain when one turns to Professor
Broad's latest book, *Religion, Philosophy and Psychical Research*.
For the philosophical argument is sandwiched with political
judgments of the most reactionary type; taut logical discussion is followed by a defence of Munich, sneers at the
workers for demanding " higher wages for less effort ", the
usual slanders about slave camps in Russia, and expressions of
contempt for democracy. Discussion on psychical research
and the evidence for the supernatural leads on to the statement
that the word " imperialism " is an emotive noise used to
express or to evoke an unfavourable reaction, but on the
same page,[1] with a logical inconsistency unworthy of so acute
a mind, he tells us that the world was a wonderful place under
the imperialisms of Rome and Britain in their heyday. And
then this piece of cynicism, just to show how analysis purifies

[1] *loc. cit.*, p. 280.

and uplifts the mind: " The world is safest for decent humane people at those rare and transitory conjunctions when a temporary equilibrium between the claims of God and Mammon has been brought about by the statesmanlike good sense of Belial."[1]

We are told that while Washington is no more than a Home for Retarded Adolescents, submission to its rule is a lesser evil than surrender to Communism, and armaments, at whatever sacrifice, offer the only chance of preventing Soviet aggression, though " I do not pretend to think that even so there is more than a slender chance of avoiding a third world war in the near future."[2]

And then the usual social defeatism. " I cannot understand how anyone with an adequate knowledge of physics, biology, psychology and history can believe that mankind as a whole can reach and maintain indefinitely an earthly paradise."[3]

Idealists and supernaturalists are all eager to assume, firstly, that man unaided by Divine Grace can never do anything worth while, and then that scientific humanism always ends up in a loss of values, a bloody anti-humanism, a trend to slavery, because it is centred on man and not God. An intrinsically sceptical, cynical and pessimistic view of human nature is at the bottom of this. The view that all human nature is somehow thoroughly corrupted and that mankind is collectively and individually in a fallen state is the only ground upon which there can be urged the necessity of redemption by supernatural means. There is no other basis on which to erect the superstructure of philosophical idealism or supernatural theology than this pessimistic view of human nature. This is the way out, and the only way out except a futile optimism, if the evils of society in decay dare not be shown to arise from a class society in dissolution.

3. Philosophy in Retreat

Meanwhile the idealism of our British universities increasingly takes the emasculated form of pre-occupation with the

[1] loc. cit., p. 180.   [2] loc. cit., p. 277.
[3] loc. cit., p. 114.

discussion of language and logic. The result on their pupils and themselves is pure scepticism, combined with a complacent delight in the mastery of their parlour game. Book after book appears, and each is more unintelligible and more completely divorced from real life than the last. Thought for these philosophers is no longer the grand instrument with which man may liberate himself from slavery to nature and social oppression, but a technique to ensure that anyone who tries to do so should be ensnared in verbal contradiction and so brought to heel.

" The realist philosophers who adopted this new programme were all, or nearly all," says Collingwood in his *Autobiography*, " teachers of young men and young women. Their pupils, with habits and characters yet unformed, stood on the threshold of life ; many of them on the threshold of public life. Half a century earlier, young people in that position had been told that by thinking about what they were doing, or were about to do, they would become likely on the whole to do it better, and that some understanding of the nature of moral or political action, some attempt to formulate ideals and principles, was an indispensable condition of engaging creditably in these activities themselves." Our contemporary philosophers on the other hand " were proud to have excogitated a philosophy so pure from the sordid taint of utility that they could lay their hands on their hearts and say it was no use at all ; a philosophy so scientific that no one whose life was not a life of pure research could appreciate it, and so abstruse that only a whole-time student, and a very clever man at that, could understand it. They were quite resigned to the contempt of fools and amateurs. If any differed from them on these points, it could only be because his intellect was weak or his motives bad."

Their pupils were told that they must not expect philosophy to be concerned with ideals to live for and principles to live by. The inference was that " for guidance in the problems of life, since one must not seek it from thinkers or from thinking, from ideals or from principles, one must look to people who were not thinkers (but fools), to processes that were not thinking (but passion), to aims that were not ideals (but caprices) and to rules that were not principles (but rules of expediency). If the realists had wanted to train up a generation of Englishmen expressly as the potential dupes of every adventurer in morals or politics, commerce or religion, who should appeal to their emotions and promise them private gains which he neither could procure for them nor even meant to procure them, no better way of doing it could have been discovered."[1]

The barrenness of such philosophising is well shown by the attitude of these philosophers in the pre-war years to the political debates which were then raging. They were asking us what we meant by such words as " democracy ", or criticising as meaningless such statements as " fascism is a menace to civilisation." Today we need not be told that these words were precisely the kind most pregnant with meaning. The willingness of men to fight for such ideas has proved no less conclusive proof of their significance than certification by analytical philosophers.

Analysis would appear to be a " sour grapes " philosophy, rationalising its own inability to think things through by denying that unsolved problems exist ; or more likely a deliberate abstraction of the mind from reality under the cloak of sharpening the instrument of reason, thus diverting thought from dangerous problems.

In either case thought is banished, and prejudice, superstition and dogmatism take its place.

4. Professor Dingle and the Poets

In a recent lecture to the P.E.N. Club on " Poetry and Science ", Professor Dingle declared that even if there had been strained relations between them in the past there is no longer any need for this. The conflict arose because " at that time it was thought that there was a real external world, the truth about which was being increasingly found out by the

[1] Collingwood, *Autobiography.*

scientists ",[1] but the philosophical background has altered and this is no longer believed. " Science is the organised description of the relations between experiences ; poetry, the expression of the experiences themselves."

Thus when a surgeon is operating for a septic appendix he is not really penetrating with his instruments that part of the external world which is his patient's body, to get hold of a very real and a very nasty infected organ and remove it, he is operating on " experiences." What we know, Dingle says elsewhere, is really " the whole content of consciousness . . . knowing a physical object is simply forming the conception of a physical object which correlates certain experiences. . . . What we know immediately is experience ; the world of material objects is what we (rightly or wrongly) infer from it."[2]

Thus whatever field we are concerned with, whether it be science, or religion, or poetry, we have nothing to go on but subjective experiences. The scientist orders these in his own way, but he no longer accepts the world of material objects. Religion organises other elements of our experience and is just as valid as science. Science cannot explain away any experience as the phantom of a diseased mind. (On the contrary it does. It distinguishes between sane thinking on the one hand and delusions and hallucinations on the other). If we take the world of material objects as real, then by contrast religious experiences may be purely subjective ; but by making experiences of physical objects subjective we make religious experiences as valid as those of the physical world. Thus the poet or theologian has just as much justification for creating a world picture that will interpret his experience as the physicist has for creating a world picture that will interpret his.

It does not seem to have occurred to Professor Dingle that this intense subjectivism places on the same plane the findings of science, the experience of the mystics, the paranoiac delusions of Hitler, and the escapist illusions of the self-deceived.

[1] Report of a Discussion on Poetry and Science, *Nature*, Jan. 16, 1954.
[2] Dingle, *The Scientific Adventure*.

Ethical values become what " we " feel to be authoritative ; but for other people quite opposite values may be just as certain. Since on his philosophy no way can be found for deciding on such a difference as to values, the conclusion is forced upon us that the difference is one of tastes, not one of objective truth. As Bertrand Russell puts it, " When we assert that this or that has value, we are giving expression to our own emotions, not to a fact that would still be true if our personal feelings were different."

Thus subjectivism leads to personal intuition as the sole criterion of truth. But as E. M. Forster remarked, " The man who believes a thing because he feels it in his bones is not really very far removed from the man who believes it on the authority of a policeman's truncheon." In both cases the belief is fundamentally irrational and has no basis in intellectual conviction.

Are we then to try to be rational about our beliefs or are we to give up the effort ? If we are to be rational we must submit our religious and ethical beliefs to severe scrutiny and, in spite of Professor Dingle, find out how to explain away those experiences which are phantoms of the diseased mind. The alternative is not the disinterested acceptance of supernatural truth, but uncritical belief, that is, credulity. Philosophy began precisely in the separation of rational enquiry from emotionally held intuition. Philosophy has ever since been unwilling to exalt convictions which are merely "experienced" to the level of convictions which can be shown to be reasonable. Hence when Dingle comes to us to display his talents, we are tempted to treat him as the citizens of Plato's Republic treated the poet, paying him reverence as a sacred, admirable and charming personage, but sending him away to another city, where his inspiration will no longer lead us astray.

CHAPTER IX

THE DEATH AND RESURRECTION OF IDEALISM

Absolute Idealism

IDEALISM reached the climax of its influence in England in the early years of the twentieth century. But it was not the subjective idealism which held that we can only know the ideas in our own minds, but the *objective* idealism which held that the object of knowledge had a real existence independent of the subject or knower, even though it was but a manifestation of the Absolute Idea. It is thus of the nature of " idea ", but is completely objective and is found and apprehended by the knower.

In the older universities the influence of Green, Bradley and Bosanquet was paramount, and elsewhere Muirhead and A. E. Taylor lent support to their doctrines. Fundamentally, this form of idealism derived from the Hegelian notion of the Absolute. The Absolute is a single unified whole, comprehending within itself all distinctions, including the distinction between mind and its objects, and embracing all differences. Our minds being but partial aspects of the Absolute take a partial and, therefore, partially false view of the universe which they contemplate, seeing it as a bundle of isolated things; it is only to the Absolute's view of itself, an inkling of which we are enabled to reach through philosophy, that the universe is revealed as a single indivisible unity.

It has often been pointed out that there are two sides to Hegel's philosophy, on the one side is the *dialectic*, the notion of change and development through the conflict of opposites— a development, moreover, which takes place in reality, in history. It was this aspect which was developed by Marx and Engels. But Hegel's philosophy can also be interpreted as a *system*, as the philosophy of a rational and unified *whole*, itself unchanging even though its appearances change, in which every part is justified in relation to the totality of which it is a part, so that the American idealist Royce could say, " The very presence of evil in the temporal order is the condition of the perfection of the eternal order." The British and American idealists accepted the static *system* of Hegel, and not his *dialectics*.

Many strange consequences follow from this doctrine. There is no real change. Change is an illusion arising from our finite point of view. " All problems and their solution exist, fully known, in the Absolute. Our procedure when confronted with a problem will accordingly be to discover the solution which already exists, not to formulate any programmes of active change."[1] Thus with the " right " philosophy, one can gather patience while the world is mad. As Barrows Dunham points out this theory had important political implications. " An eternal order of truth and righteousness is plainly just the ground on which to base existing property relations, if these are what you want to defend ; you can give them in this way a moral, legal justification, no matter how iniquitous they may otherwise appear. . . ."[2]

Absolutism in this form clearly points to the subordination of the individual to the State, and this was argued forcefully by both Bosanquet and Bradley. Later, in Austria, Othmar Spann developed it into one of the several philosophies which provided ideological support for fascism. The world is a fixed system in which all the false categories of subordination and exploitation are not passing phases but permanent forms which must be perpetuated. The individual is wholly subordinated to a static impersonal system in which he is deprived of his manhood and " self-estranged." This is Hegel without his dialectic and without his revolutionary dynamic.

Completely different was the other tendency in British

[1] Barrows Dunham, *Giant in Chains*.
[2] *Ibid*.

philosophy, represented by Bentham, Mill and Herbert Spencer. This was individualistic and liberal and reflected the earlier phase of energetic, competitive capitalism, still largely progressive, just as Bosanquet reflects the rise of monopoly capitalism and the rise of the imperialist state with its colonial aggression and state support for capitalism. Absolute Idealism, however, in spite of its reactionary character, believed in the rationality of the universe, in a purpose in existence and in the worth of man. In its way it sought to provide man with a philosophy of life, with belief in the world as a rational order in which men could work together for the common good. Bosanquet was a forward looking man if a timid one, and a reformer of a mildly Fabian type. If this seems very small beer, look at the philosophers of our own time. No longer is their message to the young men and women of our universities that the study of philosophy might make a difference to their whole lives. On the contrary they were told that philosophy was of no relevance for conduct, for an understanding of life, for developing political responsibility and political insight. It had degenerated into a kind of parlour game for over-sophisticated experts in logical finesse.

But the strange thing is that this new philosophy is really the last phase of the development of idealism itself ; it is indeed the direct successor of Absolute Idealism.

Moore and Philosophical Analysis

Moore began by *appearing* to refute idealism. Of course ordinary objects of perception exist ; the common-sense view of the world is accepted ; my body exists ; it is either in contact with the earth or not far from it ; other things having shape and size in three dimensions also exist, and so on. In making these statements Moore purported to be contradicting certain idealist philosophers who had denied them. He has therefore been regarded as a realist, in the materialist sense of believing that there exists a world with minds in it, whereas idealism believes that there exists a mind with a world in it.

Moore then goes on to say that the interesting question for philosophy is not whether his realistic statements are true. They are not only true but truisms and unquestionable. But the problems of philosophy concern what exactly one *means* when one makes one of these " true " statements such as " my body is a solid object existing on the surface of the earth." This seems unobjectionable enough ; but as we follow Moore's argument we discover that what we *mean* is that we perceive sense data or something like that, and so we are back to idealism. In fact Moore is not a realist philosopher attacking idealism. He is an anti-philosopher attacking philosophy in the interests of idealism ; for by shifting the argument from the case for or against idealism to the analysis of what one *means* by a materialist statement he pretends to escape from the vexed question of idealism versus materialism. But this escape from an important philosophical question—Moore's anti-philosophy—turns out to be a subtle way of getting back to idealism while pretending to abandon it. He has " refuted " idealism only to rehabilitate it, in a much more objectionable form.

Now this is nòt how the new philosophy appeared to those who first read G. E. Moore's *Refutation of Idealism* or his *Defence of Common Sense* (1925). These essays reflected the sudden collapse of the optimistic, one might even say the romanticist, phase of idealism, the motto of which was " All's right with the world." The cheerful confidence which regarded reality as *necessarily* ideal, which held that things *must* be good or beautiful or spiritual in order to be at all, collapsed. There emerged to refute it and supplant it the curious philosophy known as " realism "—essentially a philosophy of disillusionment.

It begins by seeking to detach the existence of things known from the act of knowing them, and in doing so it scores a number of useful points over the ordinary idealist case. It exposes the fallacy that what is experienced must have the properties of the experiencing of it. On the contrary, Moore argued, knowing makes not the slightest difference to the object. " The object, when we are aware of it, is precisely what it would be, if we were not aware." Therefore there are tables and chairs, sticks and stones, which are in no way affected by our knowing them. This looks fine and makes an immediate appeal to common sense, but what looks like common sense is often uncommon nonsense, and that happens to be so in this case. For there are a number of snags in Moore's position.

Philosophy or Anti-Philosophy ?

1. We notice first of all that these objects are what they are independently of their relations with one another, or to the world of which they are a part, or to man the knower and doer. The world therefore becomes an atomistic hotchpotch, a mere chaos in which man merely goes about observing various objects.

Now this itself is a hopelessly unscientific and, indeed, unphilosophical conception. All things are connected and affect one another ; a thing is what it is under certain conditions, and it cannot possibly be anything under no conditions at all. Moreover, while no bare mental act of awareness can affect what is known (if there could possibly be such an act), actual knowledge, which is part of our interaction with the world, our grappling with it and altering it, always does alter what it knows in a thoroughly practical way.

The trouble is that philosophers today have got into a habit of sitting about in arm-chairs contemplating patches of brown on the wall-paper, their tables and chairs (favourite objects of study), or even the ceiling. These rather passive and point-less mental activities are quite different to the kind of knowing and experiencing that goes on in a laboratory or a workshop or even when digging potatoes in the garden, and are far less likely to produce philosophical results.

2. The apparent simplicity and directness of Moore's knowledge of objects is completely bogus, for he and his disciples proceed at once, as we have pointed out, to ask a number of questions about *what you mean* when you say you

perceive a hand or a chair. Of course, says Moore, no one questions the fact that you perceive a chair and it is not the business of philosophy to say anything about your direct knowledge of that object.   The real task of philosophy is to elucidate precisely what you *mean* by such a statement, and that raises a number of problems with which philosophy has largely occupied itself for the past thirty years to the exclusion of much else of greater importance.

Russell on Perception

One can still recall the days at Cambridge when we used to fix our eyes upon the ceiling trying to discover whether or not we were directly acquainted with " whiteness " itself or only a white expanse of plaster ; whether we perceived the physical object or the sense datum (i.e. whatever is given in sensation) ; whether the sensation of white is literally part of the surface of a physical object and if so how it is related to the unsensed parts ; or whether it is *not* as a sensation a part of a physical object at all, in which case how do we reach the physical object by means of it ? Finally, whether an object is really after all a collection of sensations, of feels, whiffs, glimpses from all points of view. I remember Bertrand Russell lecturing sometime in 1915 or 1916 about what we perceive when we perceive a penny. He pulled a penny out of his pocket and held it up for us to see. We gazed at it hypnotically. He turned it over and whirled it around. We followed his every move. He explained that the penny was really a series of little eliptical flat discs, each two-dimensional, which ran out towards us like buttons on a wire. In fact, there were rows of discs running out in all directions. The collection of these was the penny. He told us the penny we saw was much smaller than the penny he saw. I confess it did not look smaller to me than pennies usually are. Then he began to say something about six dimensional space which I am afraid I did not in the least understand. Anyhow, we had somehow to get together and correlate these disc-like pennies. The collection of them was the only really-real

penny.   Though just how we were to correlate so many things
we did not possess, he did not explain.   Instead of that, he
gave the penny a final twirl in the air and put it in his pocket,
at which we all gasped.   For just what it was he was putting
in his pocket had by this time become an ineffable mystery.
I recall that Russell said on one occasion that Leibniz would
have been surprised to discover that " the end of his nose was
a colony of spiritual beings."[1]   But surely it is just as startling
to discover that the end of one's nose is a six-dimensional
manifold of Russell perspectives !

Moore and Common Sense

Now is this plain, transparent common sense ?   These
questions have been debated by the " realists " for more than
thirty years now and with no conclusion emerging.   Surely
what has happened is that so far from philosophy abandoning
a profitless task, accepting common sense without question,
and finding at last its real job, it has abandoned its real task
and bogged itself down in futility and verbiage.

When Moore says that he has no quarrel with common
sense, he says exactly what Berkeley said when he explained
away the universe as consisting entirely of perceptions—
" All the choir of heaven and furniture of the earth, in a word
all those bodies which compose the mighty frame of the world,
have not any subsistence without a mind "—but hastened to
assure us that " whatever we see, feel, hear, or anywise conceive or understand, remains as secure as ever, and is as real
as ever. . . . I do not argue against the existence of any one
thing that we can apprehend, either by sense or reflection.
That the things I see with mine eyes and touch with my hands
do exist, really exist, I make not the least question."[2]   In
fact all he is doing is to vindicate common sense which is content with this kind of knowledge, in the face of materialist
philosophers who assert the actual existence of *a material world*.

---

[1] A view which follows from Leibniz's theory of the world as
constituted by spiritual atoms or monads.
[2] Berkeley, *Principles of Human Knowledge*.

Back to Idealism

Moore is eventually driven to three possible conclusions when he seeks to tell us what we *mean* when we *rightly* say we perceive a chair.

1. We perceive sensations and there are only sensations. This is Berkeley.

2. Or these sensations *represent* a physical object which we never see directly.

3. Or the physical object is only an integrated sum of sensible apprehensions.

Now this appears to be a mere return by a roundabout route to Berkeley and Hume, after puttting up a smoke screen of " common-sense realism " to disguise what he is really after. If that is the case, he has clearly started off on the wrong foot like all the others, in spite of what he has to say about really perceiving something unaffected by our knowing. For what it is that has this objectivity turns out to be only sensations after all. The subjective idealist knew, rightly, that sensations are in the mind. Moore calls them sense data and puts them outside the mind, where they float about until sensed, like the grin of the Cheshire Cat which persisted when the cat disappeared. How clearly mental, how very much an abstraction Moore's object is, we see still more clearly when we realise that conceptions as well as perceptions hold this status, that is to say we may perceive whiteness, justice, civilisation, one-ness, two-ness and a host of other ideas which have a kind of existence which, since it is not material, is called *subsistence*. Such objects appear to be essences very much of the nature of Plato's Ideas or Forms ; they are immutable, intrinsic, and essential ; they subsist eternally in the timeless universe waiting to be lit up by our roving thoughts.

The Indefinability of Goodness

Moore's most important philosophical work was his *Principia Ethica* (1903), and here we have a very clear expression of what we are talking about. Goodness, he argues, is an indefinable quality which attaches to things independently of consciousness. It is a quality like *green* and is discovered by simple inspection, just as a colour is. " By saying that a thing is intrinsically good it means that it would be a good thing that the thing in question should exist, even if it existed *quite alone*, without any further accompaniments or effects whatever."[1]

From this it follows that all actions which in the last resort lead to consequences which are *instrinsically good* are themselves good. In other words the value of consequences can only be established by intuitions as to what is good. Thus we arrive ultimately at goods which are not themselves justified by their consequences but which are simply *good in themselves*.

To certify as " good " what inspection assures me to be good may seem, as did the perception of a chair, to be a satisfactory kind of common-sense judgment with no nonsense about it. But nothing could be more misleading. Just as our perception turned out to be something far more subjective than at first appeared, so this recognition of an *objective* good is quickly seen to be dependent upon *my* perception of it. We all know that every prejudiced judgment is felt to be the recognition of an obvious, external objective fact. The intensity of the feeling of objectivity is no measure of its actual objectivity, any more than in an hallucination. The fact that Moore is careful not to place the authority for the recognition of the good on his *feeling*, but places it on the *objective good* which he simply recognises, must not blind us to the fact that it is exactly the same thing, except for a higher degree of dogmatism.

When Dr. Malan says that the inherent superiority of white over black is not his *opinion* but an objective *fact*, which he recognises, we are on Moore's ground ; and it will be noticed that while it is possible to argue about opinions or to be brought to see that an opinion or even a conviction is not necessarily infallible or even final, one can no more argue about good as a fact, than about green as an ultimate fact of

[1] Moore *Ethics*.

experience. Moore has simply lifted ethics completely out of the sphere of genuine ethical discussion—the consideration of the worth of an act in its total setting and so on, and in doing so he has not, as many have supposed, at last put ethics on a firm foundation, on the contrary he has put an end to ethics. In much the same way when he took for granted and refused to discuss that whole series of common-sense judgments beginning with " This is a chair ", he withdrew the knowledge of the material world from the field of inquiry, leaving it therefore to uncritical dogmatism.

Richard Weaver in his book *Ideas Have Consequences*, has shown us what kind of right can be regarded as objective, unquestionable and beyond argument. He says that the right of private property is today widely felt to be a *metaphysical* right, to be recognised as absolute without reason, without justification on ground of consequences. " It does not depend on any test of social usefulness." " Private property is substance, in fact it is something very like the philosophic concept of substance." It thus constitutes an inviolable right. But having established one such right we have broken down the objection to others. " Therefore one inviolable right there must be to validate all other rights."[1]

Of course Moore is talking about the " good " and not " rights ", but the attitude is fundamentally the same, and highly significant it is politically.

Moore and J. M. Keynes

How clearly the objectivism of Moore passes over into subjectivism and how powerful and pervasive an influence that subjectivism can be, with implications running directly out to economics and politics, we can see when we consider the influence of Moore on John Maynard Keynes (the first philosopher to become a Governor of the Bank of England) and his group of Cambridge friends, which included E. M. Forster, Leonard Woolf, Hawtrey the economist, Clive Bell the art critic and other influential figures. In his *Two Memoirs*

[1] Richard Weaver, *Ideas Have Consequences.*

Keynes has a vivid autobiographical study entitled *My Early Beliefs*. Here he recounts the exhilaration and excitement caused in this circle by the teachings of Moore. The conclusion they drew, and it is significant that there was no disavowal of this conclusion by Moore who was closely associated with them, was that " nothing matters except states of mind ", chiefly their own of course, as Keynes admits—" timeless, passionate, states of contemplation and communion." It was by acknowledging the authority and ultimate nature of these states of consciousness that they achieved the salvation of their souls. " How did we know " asks Keynes, " what states of mind were good ? This was a matter of direct inspection, of direct unanalysable intuition about which it was useless and impossible to argue. . . . Victory was with those who could speak with the greatest appearance of clear, undoubting conviction, and could best use the accents of infallibility. . . . Our apprehension of good was exactly the same as our apprehension of green and we purported to handle it with the same logical and analytical technique which was appropriate to the latter."

There was of course a trick here. About the good one was merely dogmatic and authoritative, putting over a gigantic bluff ; one then gave the whole position an air of meticulous and scrupulous rationality and logical certainty by switching the whole inquiry over to the exact meaning of the propositions and statements that were used. But Keynes admits that this was really camouflage ; the real point was to carry off without question your own subjective version of the good, and here " strength of character was really much more valuable than subtlety of mind."

Keynes goes on to point out that this led to two results : individualism and a separation of experience from the external world. Goodness, he says, was now regarded as an attribute of states of mind, the life of action was of no importance here. " The life of passionate contemplation and communion was supposed to oust all other purposes whatever." This clearly indicates what Keynes called " the unsurpassable individualism of our philosophy." This attitude to life not only delivered them from the life of action (which went on all the same, but uncriticised by ethical insight and unrelated to any philosophy of life and society—went on in fact in a highly successful way, for Keynes speculated successfully in the world of finance and made a fortune), but rendered them " immune from the virus of Marxism—as safe as in the citadel of our ultimate faith as the Pope of Rome in his "—the parallel is instructive. They " repudiated a personal liability . . . to obey general rules." They " claimed the right to judge every individual case on its merits, and the wisdom, experience and self-control to do so successfully. . . . I can see us as water-spiders, gracefully skimming, as light and reasonable as air, the surface of the stream without any contact at all with the eddies and currents underneath."

Philosophy and Labour Party Economics

Keynes' attitude to material reality, therefore, became a mere traffic with surface observations and the reduction of science to probability without basic knowledge of structure or the acceptance of underlying laws as realities. As Laird says, the effect of this " was to shut nature quite out " and to deal with nothing more than a haze of probabilities. The emphasis is laid wholly on logical method and not at all on *what* nature is, as though medical science were to concern itself with treatment and not with disease. Here as in other varieties of positivism all notion of connecting with reality is abandoned. We turn away from the real environment to the mind of man who thinks about it. Such a course can only end in scepticism and irresponsibility. The linkage of data is not rooted in the rational order of the physical world but is only a logical ordering of abstract symbols. The logic has become extraneous to the factual knowledge of things, whereas it is really integral with theoretical description and part of factual knowledge. Here Keynes joins forces with all the positivists from Mach to the present day. Closely related to this was the secondary place he gave to economic theory, capitalist or Marxist. If basic understanding is impossible, nothing is left but a calculus of probability and sharp practice on the stock exchange. His famous *General Theory of Employment, Interest and Money*, which has provided the Labour Party with its current substitute for socialist economic theory, is thus merely an *ad hoc* device for dodging the worst consequences of capitalism without attempting either to understand or analyse the system. This is an elusive philosophy[1] but it is probably not so new as Keynes and his friends thought. It finds a substitute for the toilsome process of acquiring real knowledge in a form of direct perception which is intuitive as to its mode and innate as to its origin. It has but one function—vision. It therefore rejects the slow, cautious and experimental advance of scientific reason, which never claims finality and completeness, proceeding as it does not by immediate vision but by the gradual mastery of the environment. Such knowledge is always imperfect, its findings are approximations, containing some real truth, but always open to revision.

Subjectivism and Lunacy

Moore's perceived objects and perceived good—atoms of obviousness, ready made, irreducible, each clear by itself and out of all relation to other things—are really ideas, which come to take the place of material reality. This is the extreme of madness and leads to that subjectivism which is the source of a torrent of illusions and superstitions. Socially and politically it strongly reinforces an atomistic individualism blinding those who succumb to it to the positive responsibilities of the individual as the member of a social community for the lives of others than himself, and therefore cutting the nerve of democracy.

[1] It is almost identical with an obscure but influential form of idealism elaborated by Brentano, Meinong and Husserl which developed into the intensely pessimistic subjectivism of the Nazi philosopher Heidegger and the existentialism of Jean Paul Sartre. See *The Development of Idealist Philosophy from Mach to Heidegger* by Albert Fuchs in *Modern Quarterly*, Vol. 5, No. 3.

The dogmatic phase of this form of idealism is not the end ; after the period of presumption it is reduced to abdication and defencelessness, because it has no real criterion and no real content, and collapses into the opposite, the complete scepticism of logical positivism.

CHAPTER X

SCIENCE AND THE SYSTEM OF NATURE

Are we losing Faith in Science ?

BERTRAND RUSSELL said recently, " It is a curious fact that, just when the man in the street has begun to believe thoroughly in science, the man in the laboratory has begun to lose his faith."[1] This has an element of truth in it, though it is doubtful whether the average work-a-day research scientist is sceptical about the validity of *his own* science. But what is more important is the inevitable consequence of this, namely, that the man in the street will soon catch up again and *he* will begin to lose his faith in science too.

There is a widespread movement to help him lose his faith—books, broadcasts, sermons, articles in the daily and weekly press by people we think ought to know. And what is it all in aid of ? This is pretty clear. As we have seen, we must give up our faith that man can control the world in the interests of humanity, we must learn to lift our eyes unto the Heavens from which cometh our help, we must come to have more faith in mysticism than in medicine and in moral uplift than in political struggle. " Animus against science is usually animus against the political implications of that moral truth which all true science confirms and propagates. The discreditors of science are usually the seekers of social and political privilege, desperately resisting the tide of liberal effort that is quickened by science and in this defence of social privilege they are only too often supported by scholarly and other defenders of intellectual privilege, whose estate is also threatened."[2]

Do people who revolt against scientific rationalism realise that without science society must decline into small impoverished economies, such as marked the feudal past ? Faith in

[1] Bertrand Russell, *The Scientific Outlook.*
[2] Miller, *An Historical Introduction to Modern Philosophy.*

science moving from observation of empirical fact to the discovery of the laws of nature goes hand in hand with the social faith that looks to the reform of every human institution and to the establishment of genuine democracy. This is our contemporary faith in human progress, the faith that feels itself to be the master of its fate and the creative agent of a glorious future. No faith less wide or less ardent can support the tremendous effort to transform society into a co-operative commonwealth. But it is not merely the further progress of man but the continued existence of modern society that depends upon this faith. How different is this faith, based as it is on the progressive verification of its hypotheses by experiment and the growing mastery of nature, from that pragmatic " faith " which is only faith in faith, which believes because it dare not disbelieve, because there *is* no evidence. And how different is this faith in human progress, based on a profound understanding of the laws of social development, from " faith " in socialism which is self-engendered, merely emotional in origin, the expression of an unsubstantiated hope.

It is precisely the " faith " in human progress that lacks an objective basis which is everywhere tottering today, and closely linked with this is the scepticism as to the validity of science on the one hand and a growing cynicism about democracy on the other. The result is that many today are confused and misled, their confidence in the future gives way to scepticism, pessimism and moral defeatism. The science which promised knowledge of reality is said to have failed to reach objective truth, or to have provided only useful fictions which tell us nothing of what we most need to know. The vaunted movement of progress is held to be but a foolish and outmoded dogma, incompatible with a science which finds in nature either processes which run on blindly, hostile to human ideals, or an irrational sequence of events.

The Irrationalists

It will be useful to take an example or two of this corrosive scepticism before analysing this whole trend of thought. Dozens of quotations could be assembled, but the following may be regarded as typical. They represent a quite definite and very influential philosophical movement of our times.

1. T. E. Hulme's *Speculations* is the book which may be said to have set in motion the current of thought which tells us that science dissects a dead universe, that it " kills " poetry and ethics, that it falsifies our view of nature. But T. E. Hulme is also the great opponent of humanism and one of the first intellectuals to revive the dogma of original sin, of the total depravity of man. The two doctrines belong together. If science does not give us truth, truth is to be found apart from science, that is to say by religious intuition or religious authority—they turn out to be much the same. Religion assures man, dogmatically of course, not by scientific proof, that man is sinful, helpless and damned and should submit to his betters and those appointed to rule over him. That was Hulme's position.

Hulme has exerted a powerful influence on T. S. Eliot and many other reactionary writers of our time.

2. The German philosopher Vaihinger has also been popular in the anti-scientific camp. He advanced the notion of " As If." Science does not tell us about reality, it merely says that things happen *as if* such and such a fact or theory or law were so. There are no atoms or molecules but things happen *as if* there were. " It is convenient and useful to treat objects *as if* they were what in fact and in logic they are not." Science must not regard its ideas as concerned with reality itself, it only deals with co-existences and sequences. That is to say, when I heat a metal rod and it expands I must not say the heat is the cause of the expansion of the rod ; I must say " as often as I have tried the experiment the heating of the rod is followed by or accompanied by an increase in its length." This sequence follows no *law*, but it is *as if* there were a law, though in fact there is none.

Professor Woodger tells us that we must not say that all kettles boil if placed on a lighted gas ring. Such a statement is not true, it is only a useful guide to action. What we ought to say is : " If you want to boil a kettle try putting it on a lighted gas ring."[1]

3. Many of these modern statements of the irrationalist criticism of science derive from Mach, who regarded science not as a true account of the objective world but as a guide to man in the intricate maze of natural facts. This is a good example of the pragmatic fallacy, for it might well be objected that science *is* a guide in the maze of facts. Yes, indeed, but it is so because it is true and in so far as it is true, whereas Mach means that it is *only* a guide and is *not* to be regarded as true. Objectivity is eliminated, scientific results are arranged in a system or framework, with no other end in view than that of convenience and utility. Science no longer imagines itself able to sound the depths of reality, it merely seeks to achieve economy in thought by arranging facts in systems.[2]

4. Professor Ayer adds nothing new but says the same thing with the authority of the Grote Professor of Mind and Logic in the University of London. We construct scientific systems to enable us to anticipate the course of our sensations, not to discover the nature of reality. Hypotheses are merely rules which govern our expectation of future experience. " There is no sense in asking for a theoretical justification of this policy. The philosopher must be content to record the facts of scientific procedure. If he seeks to justify it, beyond showing that it is self-consistent, he will find himself involved in spurious problems."[3]

This is terrible nonsense. There is every sense in asking whether a hypothesis is justified by the fact, whether it is *true*, and every scientist does this. And surely it is precisely the business of philosophy to enquire into and state the conditions of scientific validity.

There is a distinguished company of scientists at University College ; do they, one wonders, really seek no justification in the facts for their hypotheses ? Is it not plain that the Grote Professor is really cutting the nerve of scientific research in his own university?

[1] Woodger, *Biology and Language.*   [2] Mach, *The Science of Mechanics.*
[3] Ayer, *Language, Truth and Logic.*

5. In his recent *Aquinas and Kant, the Foundations of the Modern Sciences*, G. Ardley adopts a very similar position, and once again, like Hulme, it is in support of the two-truth theory. His argument is that while theology is concerned with the truth about things-in-themselves, science is only concerned with phenomena, appearances, fictions, mental constructs. Kant lays down the sceptical premises of science, Aquinas the veridical premises of theology. He calls the method of science *categorical*, the method of theology *ontological*. Ontology gives us truth, categories give us fictions. " Modern physics is not really telling us anything of the world about us . . . it is cut off from the rest of the world and is the creation of man himself. Science in itself has no metaphysical foundations or implications (meaning it does not imply the existence of a material world, which it certainly does, J.L.). Science belongs to the categorial not to the real order." Science can therefore make no 'assertions about the nature of the real world. " It knows nothing of the constitution of nature." The world of science is a creation of the human mind ; the real world is the world of spirit.

Maritain, the Catholic philosopher, says much the same thing. " Physics lives by weaving between its measurements a web of mathematical theory and thereby elaborates a hypothetical construction. This does not correspond to the real."

Hume's Empiricism

The historical roots of these doctrines are to be found in the philosophy of Hume (1711–1776). Hume was an empiricist, that is to say a believer in the ultimacy of experienced facts and no nonsense about anything behind them. That his hard facts turned out to be mere sensations, which can be regarded as purely subjective, is of importance since it opened the door to solipsism, the view that I cannot know anything beyond my own ideas. But there are two aspects to empiricism. The second is its insistence on brute fact. It is with this second aspect that we must now deal.

This kind of empiricism is an extreme reaction from a metaphysical rationalism which believed that the intellect itself, without resort to experience of material fact, could find a great rational system that was explanatory of everything. Such a philosophy passes from the nature of thought to the nature of reality. It identifies rational ideas with reality.

Its strength is its faith in nature as an order, in reality as *one* and not a dualism of mind and matter. Its weakness is its contempt for fact, its assumption of rational order where science has not yet found a verified order, its obstruction therefore of factual scientific inquiry ; finally it easily becomes a buttress of privilege, for it consists of absolute principles, laws, ethical commands, which in practice reflect and give philosophical support to the existing order and to secular and religious principalities and powers.

The strength of empiricism is its insistence that the character of the world cannot be deduced from anything we know prior to observation, its ruthless criticism of all recognised assumptions and principles, especially those on the basis of which theology and conservative political theory is constructed. This is all to the good. After Hume we *begin with the facts*, not with assumptions, pure truths of reason, authoritative principles, intuitively perceived ultimates. All science begins here.

The weakness of empiricism is that it has to be content with individual facts and cannot pass beyond them to general laws. It ceases therefore to believe in the laws which determine and explain all events, not only in the physical sciences, but in medicine, sociology, economics and history. Reacting rightly from a rationalism which found much too easily all the first principles of theology, history, ethics, and everything else, it asserts that principles and laws cannot be reached at all. But this is scientific obscurantism, an error disastrous to science itself. If there are no valid laws then things do as they please without regard to any overall control. If things seem to behave regularly that is simply an accident. In short what we call science, the collection of observed regularities, carries no implications whatsoever regarding nature itself, offers no foothold for any forecast of the future around which purpose can weave itself.[1]

Science goes beyond Appearance

It is the paradox of science that while it is rooted in observation of facts it always passes beyond them. Science is never a catalogue of observations ; it is an *interpretation* of observations. The world of observed fact is an illusory world. The earth appears to be flat and immovable, the sun appears to be much smaller than the earth and to move round it, the stick standing in the bucket of water appears to be bent, but it is not, and so on. Science begins in the transcendence of bare fact.

Secondly, facts appear to be unconnected. The world appears to be a miscellaneous collection of bits and pieces ; it appears to be not one but many, not organised but atomistic. The scientific truth is otherwise, it links seemingly independent facts into systems. It is constantly showing how apparently unrelated facts are really dependent on one another, as when a germ in the water is found to be responsible for a typhoid epidemic.

Thirdly, facts appear to be arbitrary, a matter of chance, there seems to be no reason why they are just what they are. It turns out that they could not be otherwise. " The wind bloweth where it listeth " ; it doesn't, it blows where it has to.

To sum up : Scientific truth is frequently contrary to appearances. We do not accept brute fact, we attack it, we dissolve it, we alter it until we reach the rational, the reality behind appearances, which accounts for them, interprets them and links them in the system of nature. It is only when we know the reality beyond appearances that we obtain control over nature.

Of course the truth that we find is not above nature, is not transcendental in that sense, it is part of nature but it is beyond

[1] How ever great the number of repetitions of *b* following *a* there is not even the probability of *b* occurring the next time *a* happens.

immediate sense experience. Now empiricism, including the empiricism of our logical positivists, accepts the ultimate authority of brute fact *just as we experience it.*

It is to that extent anti-scientific. If by the authority of fact were meant the subsequent verification of a hypothesis by experiment that would be a very different matter. But this is not what empiricism means since it denies the *reality* postulated by the hypothesis, it denies the vast range of actual fact that lies beyond experienced facts.

Social Science goes beyond Appearance

The social implications of empiricism are of the first importance. The truth about capitalism is not what appears on the surface but the interpretation of these facts at the hands of a scientific economics and sociology. Furthermore, insistence on the finality of the given, the irreducibility of things as we find them, robs social reality of its potentiality, of what it is *becoming*, of what is implicit in it. It thus becomes a crude conservatism, a dogmatic defence of things as they are. The real field of knowledge in social questions as in physical science is not the given fact about things as they are, but the critical evaluation of them as a prelude to passing beyond their given form. This is the insight which Hegel brings to the enquiry into the nature of reality. The knowledge that appearance and reality are not the same thing is the beginning of truth. The mark of dialectical thinking is the ability to distinguish the essential from the apparent process of reality and to grasp their relation.

Thus the Marxist dialectic is in its first phase *negative.* As Moses Hess put it, philosophy leads " to a critique of everything that was hitherto held to be the objective truth ". Dialectic " negates " things as they are. Social reality is seen to be limited, transitory, the perishing form within a comprehensive process that leads beyond to the present form. Clearly this philosophy is a challenge to the existing order ; and just as clearly, acceptance of immediate fact as ultimate is a defence of the *status quo.*

Moreover the conception of interpretation and explanation of social fact leads at once to the idea of control and manipulation ; in other words, scientific theory is the key to freedom, while bare empiricism means accepting the facts as you find them, and so submission to natural necessity. Thus the empiricist repudiation of the truth behind the facts is coupled with a repudiation of man's claim to alter and reorganise his social institutions in accordance with his rational will.

Truth and Falsehood in Empiricism

We may now proceed to the criticism of the empiricist attack on science. This as we have seen asserts, firstly, that we can never pass beyond the facts and therefore the most we can do is to make statements about regular sequences and co-existences and formulate " laws " which are not laws but only summaries of observations. Secondly, this view allows for theories which pass beyond the data only if they are regarded as useful *fictions* and not deeper realities.

It is necessary first of all to make three willing concessions to empiricism.

1. All theory must start from fact and must be tested by fact and is concerned with the behaviour and modification of the actual material world. We repudiate all attempts to discover truth by pure reason, by intuition or by any other way than reasoning from observed fact.

2. When we pass by reason to scientific reality behind observed fact we are not passing out of the material world. The empiricist rejection of a transcendental world of non-material reality, of truths independent of material fact stands. But the rejection of such a world is not at all the same thing as the rejection of the system of nature which includes and explains the facts of observation.

3. Empiricism opposes all absolute and final truths. This is correct, but it does not imply an absolute scepticism. Because our knowledge is imperfect it is not therefore illusory ; partial truth is real, dependable truth and of the greatest importance. Truth that is always being revised is none the

less truth that we can and do often trust our lives to.   Those
who will not be content with anything less than absolute
certainty are the absolute sceptics.

Science reconstructs the facts, it does not merely catalogue
them, but the truths that it arrives at are neither *a priori*
principles nor logical deductions from the data.   In so far as
empiricism makes the point that no scientific law or theory
follows by logical necessity from the facts it is perfectly correct.
The mistake is to suppose that logical deduction is the only way to truth.

Hypothesis and the Discovery of Scientific Truth

Deductive logic can only show us what is already implied in
given premises.   Now scientific truth is not *implied* in the
data.   New truths are found by the method peculiar to science
and utterly foreign to the scholastic method of medieval
philosophy which used reason only to deduce the consequences
and implications of truths revealed by the Church, or principles
discovered by reason.   The scientific method is that of
hypothesis.   Aided by analogy and using his imagination the
scientist *guesses ;* he advances a hypothesis.   Here he follows
the philosophy of " as if ", but he draws very different
conclusions.   He says : the planets move *as if* they were
bodies moving in orbits round the sun.   The blood behaves
as if it were being pumped round the body by the heart.
These are hypotheses.   But the scientist must now proceed to
test his hypothesis.   In fact he may be said to do everything
he can to disprove it ; if he fails, it passes from the status of
as if to that of *it is so*, though of course there may be every
degree of certainty in making the affirmation.   It is *certain*
that the planets move round the sun and that the heart
pumps blood round the body.   It is almost certain that influenza
is caused by a virus which cannot be seen under the microscope.

We thus come to discover general laws and theories—for
both are hypotheses; the first a low order generalisation such
as the laws governing the expansion of gases, the second a
higher order generalisation such as the molecular theory of
gases.   The mind constantly and legitimately *passes beyond the*

data to explanations. Explanation is knowledge of wider facts accounting for a varied group of phenomena now explained as examples of *one* law, and thus knit together into a system. Thus a wide variety of facts—fermentation, decay, a festering wound, a sore throat, typhoid fever, specific plant diseases, corrosion of iron pipes—are *all* due to bacterial action.

Facts are thus constantly *revealing* other and deeper facts behind them. Empiricism is refuted by the discovery that experience always points beyond itself. Facts are the effects of realities (material realities) beyond them.

By scientific reason we grasp more and more of the ultimate nature of reality. We gain a new view of what really lies behind experience. Gradually we pass from theories covering a group of theories and from these to all embracing principles covering almost a whole branch of science, or actually uniting a number of sciences. The further we go the more coherent our system, the more facts and laws and theories don't appear to hang in the air but are *necessitated*. When we achieve this systematic understanding of nature we do not say that the order is a fiction derived from regularities in the field of observation, we say that the regularities are there because of the order or system that exists in nature.

The Uniformity of Nature

This raises a question of the first importance. How do we arrive at our belief in the existence of one comprehensive natural order embracing all things? Clearly it is not an induction from the facts, since all that we know covers but an insignificant fraction of all the order there is. The fact is that we *presuppose* a system of nature, that is why we search for order, for laws. We do not ask whether there *is* a law, but *what* the law is. However the conception arose historically, it has been abundantly vindicated by the whole growth of science over the past five hundred years. It, too, is a hypothesis, but one that is so constantly verified by the advance of science that it has come to be regarded as a postulate.

" Nothing happens without a ground, but everything

through a cause and of necessity."[1]   This is the faith of science.

1. This brings everything within the possibility of human understanding.   There is no part of nature which is incapable of being known, no phase of existence that is exempt from scientific investigation.

2. Nothing in the world is merely accidental or arbitrary. Every individual thing is an instance of a general law and every event an element in a system.   Thus mere contingency is constantly being reduced ; that is to say, things don't just happen, they are explained as necessitated and explained by being linked and united under laws and theories.   Only the fitting of a fact into a system is real knowledge.   Here the different parts of the world are united like links in a chain, *one part involves another and things hang together*.   Only this is what constitutes the intelligibility of the world.

3. Thus science is seen as a process of gradual approach to an objective set of facts already existing before all knowledge. The reality which we thus *penetrate* was there in its systematic and ordered existence before man with the power of conceptual thought existed.

4. The result of this belief is not fatalism, but a new attitude to life resulting from the power to control the world for man's benefit.

We are thus confronted with two theories of modern science. An irrationalist empiricism which is hostile to science, limits its scope and questions its validity.   It is reactionary, lends itself to the defence of the *status quo*, obstructs progress both in science and philosophy and encourages superstition and reaction.   Yet to stifle or in any way to limit scientific inquiry, and this must be the aim of the consistent empiricist, must lead to the death of any hope of finally humanising this planet.

On the other hand, " scientific theories, if properly understood, and used, serve the ends of increasing our all-round understanding of ourselves and the universe, of increasing our power to use natural processes for our own ends and our ability to organise our own social affairs ".[2]

[1] Leucippus (450 B.C.).
[2] M. Cornforth in *Philosophy for the Future.*

CHAPTER XI

FACT OR FICTION

The Philosophy of " As If "

THE philosophy of *As If*[1] has its representatives and variations both on the continent and in this country. Professor Herbert Dingle in his recent book *The Scientific Adventure* argues that all the scientist can do is to " create a world picture that will interpret his sensory experience " ; such a picture is not the discovery of scientific truth but a parable or symbol. Things happen *as if* the explanation were so, but there is not the slightest reason to suppose that it is, and any other supposition which might equally well account for the facts is just as true—or false. Professor Dingle pays theology the dubious compliment of saying that " the religious man has just as much justification for creating a world picture that will interpret his religious experience " and, one might add, just as little, for the argument really means that both science and religion are not true but fictitious.

Eddington means much the same thing when he says: " The mind has but regained from nature what mind has put into nature ", or as Vaihinger puts it : " The psyche envelops the thing perceived with categories which it has developed out of itself ".

This is simply a variant of that pragmatism which holds that science cannot get at reality but works with fictions, assumptions and hypotheses which bring order into the facts and help us to move about among them. We only *know* the facts themslves, we never reach the general law as itself a truth ; all laws and theories are only concepts, constructs of the mind. Thus the theory of evolution is not true, it is not a fact ; but fossils turn up and the limbs of animals are similarly patterned *as if* evolution had taken place. We can say no

[1] Vaihinger, *Philosophie des Als Ob.*

more. Atoms and molecules do not exist but we have the scientific results which we should expect if they did. The moment we accept atoms, forces, laws and theories as real we are becoming metaphysical, we are passing beyond the facts. Reality consists of nothing but the observed events. To quote Jeans once more : " Science has left off trying to explain phenomena and resigns itself merely to describing them in the simplest way possible. It does not matter whether the mathematical formulae in use in dealing with light correspond to any thinkable ultimate reality, which is for ever beyond the comprehension of the human mind. We are driven to speak in terms of metaphors and parables ".

Do Theories merely summarise Facts ?

Turning from an attempt to penetrate beyond the surface events to the structure of nature, empiricists like Ayer, following Mach, tell us that the sole purpose of theories is to *summarise* facts. " The most we can do is to elaborate a technique for predicting the course of our sensory experience " —not even, be it noted, the course of events in the material world, but merely what is likely to happen within the subjective world of our sensations. No light is thrown on the actual constitution and laws of physical systems ; the most that science can achieve is to predict the course of future observations on the basis of such regularities as have been observed in the past.

Now one of the uses of a true theory is that it summarises facts, but it is not true because it summarises facts; that is one of the things you do with a theory because it is true.

This substitution of utility for truth is characteristic of pragmatism which although discredited today as a system has nevertheless deeply penetrated scientific thought. Like the philosophy of *As If*, it abandons all attempts to discover the nature of reality and merely asks of any formulation or theory how *useful* it is, not whether it is true—or worse still it changes the meaning of " truth " from correspondence with reality to utility. As Dewey puts it, the truth about scientific theories lies in the fact that they help us to get things done. We are not to say that they are descriptive of objective physical processes and *therefore* they are effective in practice. Sheer effectiveness *is* their truth, or, shall we say, is a substitute for truth. As he puts it elsewhere, the truth which we formulate has no " antecedent reality ", it resides in the formulation in so far as it works. " It is not the proposition but the act of asserting it, one gathers, that is true or false. And it is true when it is the product of a competent inquiry and leads to the achievement of the goals to which that inquiry was directed."[1]

Science and Pragmatism

Thus truth is no longer the correspondence of an idea with a pre-existent fact. Any belief that we have warrant to go on asserting is " true ", even though such a warrant is something quite different from agreement with reality. It may be its utility in grafting new facts on to old, it may be because " it is profitable to our lives " or " expedient in almost any fashion ". It is in this sense that theories, constructs, hypotheses, even such " facts " as atoms, waves, cells and so forth are " true " or are accepted as working fictions.

What is so surprising about this philosophy of science is that it is so flatly contrary to the whole spirit of science. Plainly this is *not* the way that scientific work is done, even by some of those who advocate these views. It is the very opposite of science to accept a theory as true without real proof, merely because it is useful or pleasing, or even because it links new facts to old. The crazy epicycles of Ptolemaic astronomy accounted for the curious wanderings of planets among the stars by doing that, but the theory was not true. When combustion was supposed to be the escape of a fiery substance, phlogiston, from the burning substance it was found that a burned metal weighed more than the metal before burning ; the fact was that oxygen had combined with it, and so the oxide weighed more than the original metal ; but the

[1] Cornforth, *In Defence of Philosophy.*

theory that linked the new fact to the old conception was that phlogiston weighed less than nothing, so that when it escaped from the burning metal the resulting substance weighed more. It is not a sufficient test of a theory that it links up all the facts in a unified picture : false theories can do that as well as true. So far is science from accepting theories because of their merely " satisfying " qualities that scientific advance has been made precisely by excluding such beliefs and insisting on truth whether it satisfied or not.

Science clearly distinguishes useful fictions and truth. It may deliberately use one model without affirming its truth, and another accepting it as truth. Sir Oliver Lodge once wrote a book on electricity that was full of models, none of which claimed to be true, but were merely illustrative. On the other hand, modern text-books of chemistry contain diagrams or even photographs or coloured pictures of arrangements of billiard-ball-like objects which are not merely illustrative of the structure of molecules but really represent their structure.

The " ether " was advanced as a useful hypothesis, but no-one accepted it as true because it worked. Since it had been constructed to serve a special purpose, to be the medium through which light waves passed, and so on, it could not but work, having been framed for that purpose. To see whether it was true, experiments were devised.[1] These disproved its truth, but it continued to " work " ! Clearly the truth is quite different from the utility of a theory and means that it corresponds to some actual existence previously unknown. The true explanation of the behaviour of light was found in Einstein's *Restricted Principle of Relativity* in 1905. It would not have been found had utility been accepted as the criterion of a satisfactory theory instead of its truth. Utility may be based on a useful error and science is full of useful errors. Heat was for many years supposed to be a fluid—*caloric*. This theory was a most profitable one ; it was completely adequate to existing knowledge and helped to establish the science of

[1] The Michelson-Morley experiments of 1887.

heat on a firm basis. It was not for a half a century that the theory had to be given up. Now if we can clearly distinguish between the utility of theory and its truth it is clear that there is another criterion at work than utility.

Is a Theory which Works necessarily True ?

Behind this error, and behind the rather similar error that what is useful in summarising facts is as good as true because true theories do summarise facts, is a simple logical fallacy. Because a true theory works, it does not follow that every theory that works is true.

Consider the inference :

All truths are useful.
Therefore all useful beliefs are true.

Now compare it with the following inference :

Every truthful man is to be trusted.
Therefore all trusted men are truthful.

Clearly these inferences are false. The true conclusion in each case is : Therefore *some* trusted men are truthful, and, therefore *some* useful beliefs are true.

One of the disastrous consequences of believing that utility is the test of or is equivalent to truth and that we cannot and need not compare a belief with reality to see whether it is true, is the extension of the theory into the world of religion, superstition even, and into politics. The fact that science itself is held to be based on nothing sounder than the *utility* of its beliefs gives people the assurance that *any* beliefs based on their utility are as securely based as science.

But to show that a belief is useful or helpful or encouraging does not do more than explain why it is believed. Thus people go on believing in spiritualism because it consoles them for the loss of their relatives. To believe in something because it is useful merely explains why *false* beliefs are believed. True beliefs are believed not because they are useful but because we have adequate ground for believing that they correspond with reality.

Utility and Truth

There is another logical criticism of the " utility " theory. It is a fact that theories help us to summarise facts, that they are convenient and economical and so forth, *but that does not mean that they are nothing more.* If they are nothing more they are not true. Some concepts are nothing more, others are much more. If they are also true they are not a mere *product* of the need to summarise or picturise. In other words utility may be a character of truth without being its essence.

The fact is that scientific laws are not true because they are useful. They are useful because they are true, because they record in terms of thought a relation between objective facts. In scientific thinking we are conscious of reflecting upon something which exists independently of our subjective activity, which indeed puts itself into opposition in various ways to our will, something which is, in short, possessed of a nature of its own.

All these highly subjective theories of science end up by saying that we *make* truth in accordance with our needs. They surrender entirely the idea of a pre-existent world of matter with which we have to come to terms, substituting for it our sensations and experiences which we may order in any way convenient to us. There is a bit of truth in all error, and it is a fact that the knowledge of things is realised in connection with the satisfaction of our vital needs ; but this does not imply that their reality is created by subjective activity and that they exist only in so far as they satisfy those needs. Things are what they are and act according to laws which are not forced by thought upon a flux of indeterminate sensations.

The Unity of the Relative and the Absolute

The unity of the relative and the absolute aspects of truth was splendidly put by Lenin in his *Materialism and Empirio-Criticism.* " The relative limits of our approximation to the cognition of the objective, absolute truth are historically conditioned ; but the existence of this truth is unconditioned, as well as the fact that we are continually approaching it . . .

In a word every ideology is historically conditioned, but it is unconditionally true that to every scientific truth . . . there corresponds an objective truth, something absolutely so in nature." Elsewhere he says " . . . absolute truth results from the sum-total of relative truths in the course of their development, . . . relative truths represent approximate reflections of an object which exists independent of humanity . . . these reflections continually approach the truth ".[1]

The World Controllable because Determinate

Pragmatism seems to regard the world as almost completely malleable. Human works and human will can mould it to the heart's desire, can find in it, can assert about it whatever satisfies, reflects our yearnings, meets our needs. This is relativism with a vengeance. But the world is not plastic, it resents and thwarts us. This however is not to say that we cannot therefore control the material world. Quite the contrary, we can control it *because it is determinate.* The success of our theories presupposes a certain constancy of relations which we are unable to modify, a persistency in the conditions of the environment. In fact if thoughts were not the reflection of some order or system of stable relations inherent in the nature of things it would be worthless as an organ of life. As Bacon said, we modify the world up to a point if we submit obediently to it.

The pragmatic, " as if " type of theory, based on the mere utility of models, of laws summarising facts, of theories which are no more than mental fictions, really denies the basic fact that science does not order our sensations but enlarges our knowledge of nature and our practical control over it. " By rejecting the objectivity of scientific knowledge it obscures the significance of science as a weapon of enlightenment and progress."[2] This " obscures the whole function of science and confuses the issues of the fight to realise the progressive potentialities of scientific knowledge ".[3]

[1] Lenin, *Materialism and Empirio-Criticism.*
[2] Cornforth, " Logical Empiricism " in *Philosophy for the Future.*
[3] *Ibid.*

It is clear that it also opens the door for the " deception of the people by supernatural, idealistic and anti-scientific illusions ".[1]

The science which discovers the actual constitution and laws of physical systems, serves the ends of increasing our all-round understanding of the universe and of increasing our power to use natural processes for our own ends.

Pragmatism as a Reaction against Dogmatism

There is, however, a partial truth in these theories that must not be overlooked. They were in part a reaction from a dogmatic rationalism which almost identified certain limited theories of science with reality, theories which were narrowly physical or biological and sought to comprehend the whole of existence in the categories of a single highly abstract and limited department of science. Against this a philosophical humanism pointed out that our theories were man-made, partial, influenced by our desires, and often left out of account the richness, variety and obscurity of life itself. All this is very true, but the answer is not scientific scepticism. Something may escape our theories, our systems are of necessity incomplete, but the laws which the scientist formulates, though they may not exactly describe the relations of things, or comprehend all aspects of the given reality, approximate ever more nearly thereto as they become increasingly true. If there is no *absolutely certain* experimental law, there are principles which have stood the test of facts better than others, and have shown us how to render the world of experience intelligible, so that we may regard them as being relatively more certain than others.

Pragmatism leads to Dogmatism

Pragmatism came forward as the reaction against dogmatism. It reflected a profound antipathy to pedantry, system, convention, dogmatic assertion of immutable principles. In point of fact pragmatism itself leads to dogmatism. No belief is more

[1] *Ibid.*

tenaciously held or dogmatically asserted than one which we feel *needs* to be true. A recent theological controversy well illustrates this. A writer in the *Christian Century* says of a certain belief in the supernatural, " I saw that this must be either true or not true. If it be not true, then we have nothing but the confusion of naturalism. But if it be true—*and it must be true if we are to have enduring hope*—it can be true only as something revealed ".

It must be true if we are to have enduring hope : the cat is out of the bag. The foundation of all dogmatic belief is there expressed. It *must* be true because we want it to be true.

Even scientific hypotheses may be advanced on pragmatic grounds, without the necessary verification. Eddington and Whittaker are prepared to deduce the laws of nature from " eternal truths " which can be " obtained in complete perfection here and now ". Milne has argued that we may arrive at truth by rational deduction from a general principle without recourse to experience and Eddington has argued that " there is nothing in the whole system of laws of physics that cannot be deduced unambiguously from epistemological considerations "[1]

Eddington has divined that the whole system of nature is built round a number of the order 10^{78} which he called the *cosmical number*. Its existence constitutes an " eternal *a priori* truth ". This involves a startling consequence. One of the numbers of the 10^{78} group is what we may call roughly the number of *particles in the universe*. Now where are we ? " We stand in awe," says Professor Whittaker, " before the thought that the intellectual framework of nature is prior to nature herself, that it existed before the material universe began its history "[2] ; and from this we proceed to argue that the existence of such " truths " " point to a God who is not bound up with the world, who is transcendent and subject to no limitation ".

[1] See *Listener*, August 21st, 1952, and Dingle's *The Scientific Adventure*.
[2] *Listener*, August 21st, 1952.

It would be equally possible to begin with the hypothesis of the expanding universe and proceed to draw philosophical and metaphysical conclusions of the most daring kind from that.

In every case a hypothesis built on the most flimsy premises is put forward as something useful, and then a vast edifice of metaphysical and religious speculation is erected upon it. The untested assumptions of medievalism and the deductions therefrom are nothing to the dogmas which derive from the " utility " of unverified and unverifiable hypotheses.

" This kind of degenerate learning did chiefly reign among the schoolmen ; who having sharp and strong wits . . . did out of no great quantity of matter, and infinite agitation of wit, spin out unto us these laborious webs of learning which are extant in their books. For the wit and mind of man, if it work upon matter . . . worketh according to the stuff, and is limited thereby ; but if it work upon itself, as the spider worketh his web, then it is endless, and brings forth indeed cobwebs of learning admirable for the fineness of thread and work, but of no substance or profit."[1]

Do Atoms and Molecules Exist ?

The pretensions of this pseudo-scientific philosophising are convincingly exposed by taking a few actual examples of their subjective treatment of scientific concepts, for it is only by keeping the argument on an abstract level that it retains any plausibility. Consider for instance the problem of the real existence of atoms and molecules. This has been regarded by Mach and by contemporary empiricists as no more than a mental construct which conveniently explains or renders intelligible certain facts or recorded observations. But every laboratory worker believes in the objective existence of atoms and molecules (which is quite a different thing, by the way, from saying exactly *what* an atom, for instance, is). Particles in suspension in a liquid can be graded from those which settle in a fine deposit to those that remain permanently in suspension

[1] Francis Bacon, *The Advancement of Learning.*

and are invisible under the microscope ; that they are there becomes apparent if they are illuminated by a cross beam of light as motes are rendered visible in a sunbeam, or they may be precipitated as a deposit by centrifugal force. A colloidal solution of gold behaves like this, showing a neat transition from the unobservable and hypothetical to the visible. The virus was invisible until photographed, but never *seen* directly, under the electron microscope. Yet invisibility is often, rather naively, taken as evidence of non-existence.

Interesting work has been done with fine films from 20 to 100 molecules thick in comparison with still finer films only one or two molecules thick. The difference in behaviour follows from what one would expect from actual molecules so arranged. The existence and behaviour of liquid crystals is explicable in terms of the behaviour of actual molecules. They can be broken up, but the molecules rejoin. We thus obtain a curious and exciting combination of liquid form and permanent shape. All living cells in the body contain such liquid crystals.

Radio-active isotopes which after passing into the body enter the structure of some of the proteins of the brain or muscles in a few minutes, replacing other atoms which step out, are actual entities giving manifest signs of their presence, not figments of the mind.

Even the electron is now established as a physical entity. Wilson's cloud-chamber has shown that when ionisation is produced by X-rays or electrons in a gas with water-vapour present, cloud is formed about the ions (just as mist or raindrops are formed). This, followed by suitable measurements and calculations, made it certain that bodies much smaller than the smallest atom were present.

The television set, with its cathode ray tube, and the electron microscope have made the concrete existence of electrons quite plain to the most critical intelligence. A development of Wilson's cloud-chamber method has made it possible to take camera pictures of the paths of alpha-particles, each of which is identical with the nucleus of a helium atom. Electrons are deflected by the electro-magnet, a fact which is the basis of the electron microscope—another indication of the materiality of electrons.[1]

The molecular structure of crystals has been demonstrated by the diffraction effects of their lattice-like arrangement, on X-rays. Molecular structure and the arrangement of the molecules is the explanation of the different properties of materials such as glass, iron, cotton, silk, rayon and wool.

But we should not limit our attention to the sub-microscopic world. No scientific fact is *directly* known. It is impossible to separate the sequence of observations from the train of judgments, which follows, or to imagine observations that are not suggested and directed by existing knowledge. Fact and theory cannot be so easily divorced. *Is* the earth an oblate sphere with a radius of 6,370 kilometres or do we merely agree to act *as if* it were? Are the plant body and the animal body made up of cells? These things are indeed true, but these are not facts open to immediate inspection.

What Mach wanted to eliminate, namely the atom, has proved the turning point of modern physics. Nor is it that the theory has merely proved useful in its consequences. The knowledge that matter consists of atoms is much more important than all the " consequences of the picture ". Progress has not followed the procedure of regarding atoms as fictions but taking them as real things to investigate. The fact that molecules do not break down into smaller portions of the same " stuff ", but into quite different substances, e.g. copper sulphate, a blue crystalline substance, into copper and sulphur and oxygen, and that an atom itself breaks down not into little bits of atoms but into something quite different from an atom, should not disturb anyone. Particles having determinate qualities of their own can make up bodies having quite different

[1] Perhaps one cause of doubts as to the material existence of atoms and electrons is the confusion of materiality with solidity. Material reality is that which exists independently of mind. It is not necessarily solid. Light is material, but it is not solid. No-one today holds the billiard ball theory of the atom, but the electrical theory of the atom does not lessen its materiality.

special qualities. What is electricity at one level may be ordinary solid substance at another.

Science and Witchcraft

There is always the possibility of distinguishing between constructions which are knowledge, and constructions which are only plausible fictions. Our imaginary constructions cannot, beyond a certain point, be used to anticipate correctly the results of our actions ; therefore they cannot be valid. When Professor Polanyi declares that it is impossible to find a satisfactory argument to persuade the Azande of the Southern Sudan that witchcraft is not responsible for the smelting of iron ore going wrong in a particular case, our reply is that witchcraft has not given the Azande steadily increasing control over the process of smelting as science has with us. The purely fictitious, however specious and pleasing, does not increase our control over nature, it prevents further advance. Professor Evans-Pritchard, the anthropologist, feels under no obligation to instruct the Azande[1] in the folly of witchcraft. On the contrary he feels that " it provides them with a philosophy of events which is intellectually satisfying ", and that " what at first sight seems no more than an absurd superstition is discovered by anthropological investigation to be the integrative principle of a system of thought and morals and to have an important role in the social structure ".[2] How would Evans-Pritchard, feel, however, about calling in a witch doctor to deal with his wireless set or his car or cope with a difficult virus infection in his child ?

I have no doubt that the aim of this undermining of science is not to harm science at all, though that may be its effect. It is to demonstrate that science has no right to close the door to belief in the supernatural. It is to this conclusion that every argument leads. But it should be noted that it does not merely open the door to orthodox theological beliefs which may claim to be rational, but to any and every superstition,

[1] Evans-Pritchard, *Witchcraft, Oracles and Magic among the Azande.*
[2] Evans-Pritchard, *Social Anthropology.*

since they are all validated by the principle that whatever hypothesis is useful is as valid as any scientific theory. Professor Polanyi is quite explicit about it—you *choose* your system of beliefs, and what you choose is really a whole tradition, a closed system of assumptions and practices ; this is what the Church is, and this is what science is. If you feel at liberty to profess your faith in the arbitrary and imaginatively constructed fictions of science, you are also at liberty to accept the dogmas, miracles and practices of the Church. Above all, he says, we must learn to *abandon the critical obsession and acquire the capacity to hold beliefs.*

One effect of such views is to remove social institutions from scientific enquiry, to limit science to finding ways and means to accomplish the ends settled by a society based firmly on uncriticised dogmas. Yet what is wanted is the application of scientific methods to society itself and its institutions, and to the task of establishing satisfactory ends. The former method leaves the most important things to decision by custom, prejudice and class interests and by tradition embodied in institutions which serve only minorities.

Only a clear understanding that science is capable of discovering the nature of reality, physical, psychological, economic, social and political, will give us the confidence to use and *extend* scientific methods, in preference to irrational beliefs, to obtain our understanding and control over nature and society.

CHAPTER XII

MARXISM AND THE CHANGING WORLD

Marxism as a Theory of Knowledge

ONE of the most fundamental questions in philosophy is what we understand by knowledge and how valid is our knowledge of reality. Clearly this is of the first importance for science. Marxism, as a theory of knowledge, rejects the *a priori* approach of the older rationalists, who thought that the mind could discover truth not contained in or derived from our actual experiences, truths which revealed the nature of reality and were found by the mind working on its own account. But Marxism also rejects the method of knowing which bases everything on passive reception of sense impressions and the building up of these into concepts, laws and so on.

Nevertheless both rationalism and empiricism contributed much to scientific understanding. "The Greeks had shown that you can get to know the world by thinking about it. The early moderns had shown that you can get to know the world by sensing it. There remained the chance to crown all this by showing that you can get to know the world by acting on it, where the phrase ' acting on it ' means the carrying out of a programme based upon an entire relevant theory."[1] That is to say, action proceeds from valid theory, and is successful to the degree that theory reflects reality. The combined constructions of sense and intellect thus become a way of controlling it.

The Marxist theory of knowledge requires logic, sensation and practice. " It seems plain that we must have all three, and that theories of knowledge have very often suffered from fastening exclusively upon one of the parts. Mere empiricists cannot account for generalisations. Mere rationalists cannot tell whether their deductions correspond with fact. Mere

[1] Barrows Dunham, *Giant in Chains.*

pragmatists cannot know what it is their practice confirms."[1]

Ideas arise in the human mind as it grapples with a changing but objective world. The objectively existing state of affairs is reality, the mental reflection which is never perfect is knowledge. In so far as this knowledge apprehends reality, it is absolute ; in so far as it is partial and conditioned by the limitations of our point of view, it is relative. Knowing therefore is a process of gradual approach to an objective set of facts already existing before all knowledge.

The Dialectical Method

The dialectical method involves the consideration of things in terms of their change, development, evolution. If all things are in development then we must recognise that the ultimately important thing is not the " state " in which the subject matter happens to appear at a given moment, but the rate, direction and probable outcome of the changes which are taking place. We must operate in terms of a methodological perspective which not only takes account of the fact that changes are taking place, but also prepares for a precipitation of new qualities and modes of behaviour.

Professor Herbert Dingle describes dialectical materialism in the following terms : " Certain principles are stated to be inevitably operative in community life and it is then deduced that these principles must operate also in the realms of physics and biology. The conclusion is that the laws of matter must be derivable from the laws of human communities, and that all this constitutes science ".[2]

It is amazing how a person holding an important academic position can have the effrontery to falsify a philosophical position which even those who reject Marxism must at least regard as important. It also betrays a lack of intellectual integrity which we would not find if Professor Dingle were examining and endeavouring to refute almost any other philosophical theory from Cartesianism to Posivitism.

[1] Barrows Dunham, *Giant in Chains.*
[2] Dingle, *The Scientific Adventure.*

Mr. Douglas Garman has rightly characterised this as " one of the most shameful phenomena of the long and gloomy twilight of liberal humanism ".[1]

The travesty of Marxism of which Professor Dingle is guilty is contradicted by the plain exposition of dialectics as we find it in the works of Marx and Engels and their successors. " Not a single principle of dialectics can be converted into an abstract scheme from which, by purely logical means, it would be possible to infer the answer to concrete questions ". The laws are to be regarded as " a guide to activity and scientific research, not a dogma ".[2]

" Genuine dialectics ", Lenin wrote, " proceeds by means of a thorough, detailed analysis of a process in all its concreteness. The fundamental thesis of dialectics is : there is no such thing as abstract truth, truth is always concrete."[3]   Engels devotes many pages to the scientific evidence which forces every objective thinker into a dialectical as opposed to a metaphysical (i.e. static and mechanical) approach. " To me " he says, " there could be no question of building the laws of dialectics into Nature, but of discovering them in it and evolving them from it."[4]   " The revolution which is being forced on theoretical natural science by the mere need to set in order the purely empirical discoveries, great masses of which are now being piled up, is of such a kind that it must bring the dialectical character of natural events more and more to the consciousness even of those empiricists who are most opposed to it."[5]   " Nature is the test of dialectics, and it must be said for modern natural science that it has furnished extremely rich and daily increasing materials for this test."[6]

That is indeed so, and the whole development of science since the days of Engels has abundantly substantiated his recognition of the dialectics of nature.

[1] *Modern Quarterly*, Vol. 3, No. 3.
[2] *Bolshaya Sovetskaya Entsiklopedia*, Vol. 22, p. 155.
[3] Lenin, *One Step Forward, Two Steps Back*.
[4] Engels, *Anti-Duhring*.
[5] *Ibid.*
[6] *Ibid.*

It is this natural fact of development, change and process that has outmoded the logic of self-identity, often though not justly, attributed to Aristotle. The logic which regards a thing as persisting in its defined properties under all conditions and independently of its connections with other things is the *metaphysical* attitude, which derives from the scholasticism of the Middle Ages.

The Meaning of Metaphysics

The dialectical method of thought stands in such sharp contrast to the metaphysical that it may be worth while elaborating a little on the distinction. The term metaphysics has three principal meanings :

(*a*) It can mean the study of the ultimate nature of things, as contrasted with the particular sciences. Materialism and idealism are, in this sense, metaphysical systems.

(*b*) It can refer to speculations or doctrines concerning matters beyond human experience and incapable of verification. Such "metaphysics" is mystical and reactionary and tends to deny, belittle and prevent scientific knowledge of the world and man.

(*c*) Metaphysics means to Marxists a method of approach " which sees in nature an arbitrary collection of objects and events, independent of and isolated from one another, without universal and basic relationships ".[1]

The metaphysical approach was not always indefensible. It was historically conditioned by the level of knowledge of its day. Science could not advance until nature had been parcelled into clearly defined entities each with its precise properties. But this method of study grew into the tendency to consider these properties as completely known and unalterable. " To the metaphysician, things and their mental images, ideas, are isolated, to be considered one after the other apart from each other, rigid, fixed objects of investigation given once for all."[2]

To treat human nature, for instance, as something unalterable, above all to treat the form it takes under specific historical

[1] Rosenthal and Yudin, *Short Philosophical Dictionary*.
[2] Engels, *Anti-Duhring*.

and social conditions as revealing its absolute and unalterable essence, is to be metaphysical in this sense. The fixity of species in biology, the permanence of economic laws, the fixed nature of capitalism, of democracy, of war, are other examples of metaphysical thinking.

Dialectics, on the contrary, sees things as possessing properties dependent upon the conditions under which they are found, and as undergoing development and change. It sees in all phenomena something struggling into existence and something dying away. This may be true of a developing human character, of an economic system, of society as a whole as capitalism declines and socialism develops.

The Deficiency of Formal Logic

It was Francis Bacon who first saw the inadequacy of formal logic from the scientific point of view because it placed emphasis and centred attention on the static.

" It cannot be that axioms established by argumentation can suffice for the discovery of new works, since the subtlety of nature is greater many times over than the subtlety of logic."

For twenty-five centuries we have tried to work down from abstractions rather than up from tangible events. The philosopher, or even the scientist, who is obsessed with formal logic evidently regards abstractions as real things. The process is obviously inside their heads and there insulated.

Consider the " law of thought " known as the principle of identity. " A is A and not not-A." A fish is a fish and nothing else. Ice is ice. Now the simple truth about such laws is that in any particular argument in which certain terms are being used, each term having been once defined, must be used consistently in the same sense. You cannot *state* that A is B, if you start by saying A is A. People do as a matter of fact change the meaning of a word in the course of an argument and this trick or fallacy has constantly to be exposed. But is a statement about the consistent meaning of a term a statement about *existence* ? That is another matter altogether.

If a fish grows lungs and comes out of the water is it a fish ?

If ice melts, is it ice ?   In *fact* a thing can be both A and not-A at the same time.   It is here and here only that logic of the Aristotelian type breaks down.   The kind of statement that would adequately reflect a changing thing would have to be more flexible.

But there still remains a real meaning to the law of identity even in such a process of change, for the law simply means that (*a*) there are constancies in the world and (*b*) change itself is inconceivable without reference to something constant.

There are constancies in the world.   The modern scientist does not deny constants and uniformities, but he finds them in relations and processes instead of in essences and lumps.

A certain pattern of action going on on the sub-atomic level *is* an atom of a particular character and is invariably so. Granted a certain combination of elements, or association of conditions, a metal rod expands, or a current of electricity is generated.   This is certain and can be relied upon.

Change requires the non-changing.   There can be no evolutionary change unless *something* is changing and developing.   That *something* is obviously something persisting. When an egg hatches into a chicken, or an eohippus with four toes and the size of a fox evolves into a horse with one toe, there is not only change, but identity, or evolution would be meaningless.   I am certainly a very different person from what I was twenty-five years ago, yet in a very real sense I am the same person and I am entitled to stick to my birth certificate and identity card.

The scientist therefore, and the man in the street who wants to be objective too, when he says that *a thing is what it is*, and nothing else, should remember melting ice cream, exploding rockets, developing lung fish, pigs that may be piglets, boars or sows, eggs that may be edible, addled or just on the point of hatching, water which may be hot or cold, mushrooms that are growing fast, men and anthropoid apes, different but united in a common ancestor.

But let him also remember that in any scientific discourse terms must be inviolable, which does not mean that a scientist cannot draw our attention in such a discourse to the changing character of what he is talking about, whether this be amphibians, democracy, liberty, or simply eggs.

Above all let us beware of hypostasising abstractions, that is to say deriving quite correctly a general term from the facts and then persuading ourselves that the term has a meaning in itself and stands for something eternal and independent of the facts, perhaps even trying to create facts to correspond to it. This is the great vice of all ideologies, especially in ethics and politics.

Ever since Plato lifted philosophic thought into the world of eternal and immutable " ideas " human thinking has suffered from a shortage of oxygen.   George Henry Lewes said that " even a great intellect may unsuspectingly wander into absurdities when it quits the firm though laborious path of inductive inquiry ".

But the answer to this danger is not to study merely the form of thinking while disregarding the matter, hoping to rise superior to science.   Thought must be the instrument of science, neither its master nor independent of it.   When men use their hands and minds in the discipline of science, of art, music, politics, their knowledge and well-being advance. When they use their minds for establishing eternal laws and principles in philosophy, economics, jurisprudence, politics, then the good life is hindered and turned to evil.

Aristotle

Aristotle's logic became, in the Middle Ages, the perfect instrument of metaphysical thinking.   But if we consider Aristotle in relation to his own times, we shall find less to quarrel about in his philosophy, and if he were alive today probably the last thing in the world he would be is an Aristotelian.

Aristotle conceived matter as aspiring and moving towards a higher, more active and creative principle, so that concrete reality possesses an inalienably dynamic aspect. " This undoubtedly dialectical conception must be noted as a very high point reached in the development of philosophic and scientific thought in Greece."[1] Nevertheless although the body changes and matter changes, he held that form exists eternally.

A mechanical attachment to Aristotelian logic under twentieth century conditions represents a denial of dialectics in favour of formalistic thinking. " Although it contains metaphysical elements, Aristotle's logic, by virtue of its deep rooted connection with the scientific developments of his epoch and the whole process of knowledge, cannot be called formal logic in the bourgeois sense. Aristotle did not place the logical forms of investigation in any opposition to their concrete content. On the contrary he tried to elicit the logical forms and connections from the basic characteristics of existence. It is this which explains the living depth of his analysis, and the acuteness of the dialectical conception of problems . . . He was the first to clarify the laws and forms of logical inference connecting them with all fields of knowledge —natural science, politics, ethical ideals ".[2]

[1] Alexandrov, *Aristotle* (Moscow).
[2] *Ibid.*

CHAPTER XIII

MAN AND NATURE

Man a Part of Nature

THE whole of modern science works steadily in the direction of the Marxist interpretation of man and society. When the theory of evolution was established and subsequently the early stages of man's development were elucidated, a heavy blow was struck at the view that man stands over against nature as somehow belonging to another world.

Nature is such that man has evolved in the course of time, whatever his antecedents or causes ; and man like everything else, once he appears, is part and parcel of nature ; yet he is different from the rest of nature and for that reason is not to be contrasted with an alien world because he distinctively differs from everything else in his surroundings, or because much in nature may be felt to be hostile to his purposes. Certain things in nature threaten man's security, others sustain his projects. The world is not alien to him though it surrounds him with uniformities. Indeed without such uniformities he would be helpless. Freedom is a knowledge of necessity, and the more man understands the laws of nature the more he is able to control his environment. " The relations between man and his environment are both internal and external, also ; that is to say, man and environment modify each other. To the extent that men singly and collectively modify their environment they are ' free ' ; to the extent that their environment modifies them, they are determined. It seems plain enough that men aren't absolutely free or absolutely determined . . . strange to say, men need the determinateness of the world (and of their own nature) in order to be free. Their ability to satisfy their wishes is in proportion to their technology, their technology is in proportion to their knowledge, and their knowledge depends upon regularity of pattern in events. At the same time, events do get altered by human action, and therefore reflect the ' free ' causality of man. Thus free will and determinism are theories which are not only compatible but necessary to each other. Taken dialectically, they together perfect one's vision of the world."[1]

Is Nature Hostile to Man?

To the scientist nature as it exists outside man appears first of all to be absolutely impersonal ; it assists no one, it hinders no one, intentionally. Nature is the source and substance of life—to be enjoyed and used by those who take the trouble to understand its laws. Nature in itself has no morality. But this is only a superficial view, though it is truer than any primitive personification of nature as a beneficient force working for man's good ; the profounder view is that man has now been for so long interacting with nature that the whole surface of the planet has been profoundly modified, it has become an artifact of cultivated fields, mines, timber forests, ways of communication, stone and brick built up into cities and a thousand natural forces harnessed by man.

The old religious notion that man had been created and put into the world has given way to the understanding that man himself has a natural history. Man is nature ; man is nature coming, slowly, painfully, haltingly, to awareness of its own meanings and uses. Man is not something placed in nature. He gathers up the scattered threads of process and meaning. He is nature passing critical and creative judgment upon her own processes and selecting this, rejecting that—making a world ever nearer to his heart's desires.

Marxism considers the world not as something finished, to be judged now as good or bad. We face a future—*the unfinished business of existence*. Nature is not only the scene of man's exploits, it is itself the exploit ; it is human life emerging from the primitive past, out of its degradations and its fears,

[1] Barrows Dunham, *Giant in Chains*.

and achieving freedom and rationality and beauty, by its growing understanding, by its intelligent acceptance of its materials, and by its artistic remoulding of those materials to new levels of beauty and use.

" Nature has produced, supported and sustained human civilisation. For man is a part of nature, carried on by her forces to work the works of intelligence. In him she bursts forth into sustained consciousness of her own evolution, producing in him knowledge of her processes, estimation of her goods and of her ultimate significance. Without such creatures as man nature might well exist, but she would exist unvalued and unobserved. You cannot add man as some extraneous figure, for he has grown out of nature's own stuff and been wrought in her workshop. He is no mere commentator on the world or spectator of it. He is the supreme instance where nature has evaluated herself."[1]

Man himself a Revelation of Nature's Possibilities

What is the philosophical significance of this ? Can nature mean the same thing after man's creative activity as apart from him ? Man is surely an illustration of what nature is, in its potentiality. He reveals nature. This is the lesson of the whole history of philosophy. Thinking about man and thinking about nature have always gone together. We are coming to realise that the world is something out of which something can be made. And to make something out of it is what everything is bent on doing. Nature is not a creation but the challenge and opportunity to create. In fact we cannot characterise the nature of the world until we have man before us. The nature of any process is only revealed in the process as a whole and the world is not complete without man and his knowledge.

Social Change and Economic Production

Science therefore proceeds from an examination of the physical and biological world to an examination of man as a

[1] Woodbridge, *Nature and Mind.*

social being, man interacting with the physical world and creating at first primitive society and subsequently civilisation. We see society in continuous change and in the laws of change and the direction of development we discover both our limits and our opportunities. Society moves and it is quite untrue that human relationships are essentially the same today as they were thousands of years ago. But what are the basic causal factors and consequent general direction of the evolution of human society ? The changes that concern us most are those in the mode of sustaining life, in the system of economic production. When this changes we may expect corresponding changes in every other department of social life, changes moreover which are far from automatic, involving vigorous struggle between those groups of people having a common economic relationship to the means of production bestowing valuable privileges and the power of exploitation, and those other groups whose position is inferior. The interests and whole way of life of these groups is bound up, either advantageously or disadvantageously, with a certain mode of production and system of property relations, and here is the real motive either for perpetuating or changing the system. Man has made his history not by following the star of an abstract ideal or by walking on a line of preconceived progress. He has made it by creating his own conditions, that is to say, by creating through his labour an artificial environment, by developing successively his technical aptitudes and by accumulating and transforming the products of his activity in this new environment.

As we look back over the great social transformations of the past, the development of tribal into ancient slave society, slave society into the medieval system based on serfdom, the feudalism of the Middle Ages into capitalism, with the concomitant modifications of institutions and cultural life, we see in each case essentially the same dynamic pattern, the concrete exemplification of a mode of economic production which has outlived its usefulness and which is already being transformed into a new mode, held back from completely establishing itself by the vested interests of those classes which are bound up with the old. In this struggle we see the enormously important part played by ideologies both in defending and attacking the old regime, especially when that regime believes passionately in its own legitimacy and in the ethical justice of its privileges. It is in such moments of transition that ruling philosophies which once served the cause of progress change their character and are subtly modified to serve the cause of reaction, the class concerned now having lost its progressive role and become an obstacle to social advance.

Idealism and the Industrial Revolution

This is well shown in the development of idealism in the nineteenth century. The more developing industrialism showed its cruel side, the more did idealism seek to prove that somewhere, somehow, the world is good and is working for what man is working for and cares for the objects of his care. The more the world of science and economics was seen as merely mechanical and revealing only the blind interaction of dead entities, the more necessary was it to prove that the world of science was a mere show world, and that behind it, underneath it, permeating it, lay the real world, a very different kind of thing. That real world was shown to be not mechanical, not a blind aimless process, but spiritual and moral, guaranteeing the outcome of man's endeavours. Such a philosophy is a socially conservative force. It seeks to show that society is really serving the highest ends when all the evidence points in the opposite direction. Thus Bosanquet says, " On the view here accepted, finiteness, pain and evil are essential features of Reality, and belong to an aspect of it which leaves its marks even on perfection. If we knew everything and could feel everything we should see and feel what finiteness, pain and evil mean, and how they play their part in perfection itself. Therefore we shall try to understand the world and co-operate with it rather than remould it."

Mind and Social Change

Ideas, then, may be positive or negative in their effect, but nothing happens without them. It is a travesty of Marxism to assert that it sees social life as wholly determined by unconscious economic forces and mind as a mere glow of derived and ineffectual consciousness on the surface of material events. No single step in social evolution, from the fabrication of the first tool and the organisation of the first social tasks to the great clash of ideologies in our time in which the social struggle is being fought out, can take place without the formulation and activity of ideas.

Mind emerges out of its natural origins slowly, through the ages. A chief instrument in this release of mind into its own areas of freedom has been language. In developing the forms and the contents of social communication, mind comes to grasp its own possibilities and to create the great instrument of modern science and finally of scientific sociology.

The intellectual life may become a pedantic intellectualism, cutting itself off from its natural roots in experience, and boasting its high, sterile lineage ; or it may become social-intelligence, gathering into itself understanding of the world and of the laws of social development. Philosophy becomes no more than an instrument of social obstruction or a negative diversion serving the same end of frustrating constructive effort unless it is rooted in these social processes by which the world is creating and recreating itself, age by age. We do not know the meaning of life, however profound our mystical insight or soaring our metaphysical speculation, if we do not know how to remake the world, how to take hold of the forces of change and put ourselves in line with the law of historical development. Then every step may provide a fulcrum for new leverage, if only the need be felt, and the courage can be aroused, and the intelligence can be released.

But the hardest lesson philosophy has to learn is that this understanding does not come to the detached scholar in his study or to the saint on the mount of vision, but only to him who is in the midst of the struggle and has taken sides with

" the class that holds the future in its hands."   Society itself
discovers the cause of its destined evolution and asserts itself
to proclaim the laws of its movement.   Here Marxists differ
from all other kinds of socialists.   The ideals of the earlier
reformers and the theories of those who reflected on society,
although they reflected the class struggle " with a lofty sense
of justice and a profound devotion to an ideal, nevertheless
reveal ignorance of the true causes and of the effective nature
of the antithesis against which they hurled themselves by an
act of revolt spontaneous and often heroic.   Thence their
utopian character."[1]   That is why all earlier movements
ultimately flagged and failed, while the proletarian movement
of today is marching forward.   The reason is " the change of
society in its economic structure ;   it is the formation of the
proletariat in the bosom of great industry and of the modern
state.   It is the appearance of the proletariat upon the political
scene—it is the new things, in fine, which have engendered
the need of new ideas.   Thus critical communism is neither
moraliser, nor preacher, nor herald, nor utopian—it already
holds the thing itself in its hands and into the thing itself has
put its ethics and its idealism."[2]   It is the consciousness of
this revolution and especially the consciousness of its diffi-
culties.   It explains to us the necessity, the birth and the
development of warring classes as a fact which is not an
exception, but the very process of history.   " Ethics and
idealism consist henceforth in this, to put the thought of
science at the service of the proletariat."[3]

Idealism and Social Decay

Social idealism has so far only confronted an alien world
with ideals too high for it.   But to hold rigorously to what is
not possible in the kind of world in which we find ourselves
is a mark, not of exalted morality, but of immature folly that
has not yet discovered what morality really is.   Morals are

[1] Labriola, *In Memory of the Communist Manifesto.*
[2] *Ibid.*
[3] *Ibid.*

not prior to existence, nor is it sufficient to believe in them but not to practice them ; such ineffectual ideals are of little value for the guidance of men in the present situation.

Modern idealism is increasingly aware of its futility, its subjectivism. As Professor Mackinnon says of the Church, and it is true of all idealistic movements, " It simply does not possess the forces necessary for such a task." Its understanding " is simply not adequate to the perplexities of the present." " It is the prisoner of the total situation in which it is involved."[1] Thus idealism, whether philosophical or ethical, has become a symptom of decay, failing to perceive that its judgment on the contemporary situation reflects its own subjective mood, its own futility and powerlessness. Such idealists are to be pitied. Nevertheless they are a danger, for they are the carriers of a poison which will destroy us if the infection is allowed to spread.

As Herzen so well described them : " They are not the doctors of a sick society, as they imagine, they are the disease."

[1] Mackinnon, *Christian Faith and Communist Faith.*

INDEX